Editor
Eric Migliaccio

Editor in Chief
Karen J. Goldfluss, M.S. Ed.

Cover Artist
Barb Lorseyedi

Illustrator
Mark Mason

Art Coordinator
Renée Mc Elwee

Imaging
James Edward Grace

Publisher

Mary D. Smith, M.S. Ed.

Grade 4

Project-Based Writing

- Pre-made & customizable units
- Multi-genre lessons & projects
- Targeting 21st-century skills
- Technology-based lessons
- Cross-curricular connections
- Guided by student choice

Teacher Created Resources

Author

Heather Wolpert-Gawron

For information about Common Core State Standards, see pages 4–5 of this book or visit *http://www.teachercreated.com/standards*

Teacher Created Resources
6421 Industry Way
Westminster, CA 92683
www.teachercreated.com

ISBN: 978-1-4206-2782-4

© 2014 Teacher Created Resources
Made in U.S.A.

Table of Contents

Table of Contents *(cont.)*

Common Core State Standards

Project-Based Writing, Grade 4 gives students and teachers the necessary resources and ideas needed in the process of creating project-based-writing units in the classroom. During each step of this process, students will engage in activities that meet one or more of the following Common Core State Standards. (©Copyright 2010. National Governors Association Center for Best Practices and Council of Chief State School Officers. All right reserved.) For more information about the Common Core State Standards, go to *http://www.corestandards.org/* or visit *http://www.teachercreated.com/standards*.

Informational Text Standards
Key Ideas and Details
ELA.RI.4.1. Refer to details and examples in a text when explaining what the text says explicitly and when drawing inferences from the text.
ELA.RI.4.2. Determine the main idea of a text and explain how it is supported by key details; summarize the text.
ELA.RI.4.3. Explain events, procedures, ideas, or concepts in a historical, scientific, or technical text, including what happened and why, based on specific information in the text.
Craft and Structure
ELA.RI.4.4. Determine the meaning of general academic and domain-specific words and phrases in a text relevant to a *grade 4 topic or subject area*.
ELA.RI.4.5. Describe the overall structure (e.g., chronology, comparison, cause/effect, problem/solution) of events, ideas, concepts, or information in a text or part of a text.
Integration of Knowledge and Ideas
ELA.RI.4.7. Interpret information presented visually, orally, or quantitatively (e.g., in charts, graphs, diagrams, time lines, animations, or interactive elements on Web pages) and explain how the information contributes to an understanding of the text in which it appears.
ELA.RI.4.8. Explain how an author uses reasons and evidence to support particular points in a text.
ELA.RI.4.9. Integrate information from two texts on the same topic in order to write or speak about the subject knowledgeably.
Range of Reading and Level of Text Complexity
ELA.RI.4.10. By the end of year, read and comprehend informational texts, including history/social studies, science, and technical texts, in the grades 4–5 text complexity band proficiently, with scaffolding as needed at the high end of the range.
Foundational Skills Standards
Text Types and Purposes
ELA.RF.4.3. Know and apply grade-level phonics and word analysis skills in decoding words.
ELA.RF.4.4. Read with sufficient accuracy and fluency to support comprehension.

Common Core State Standards *(cont.)*

Writing Standards

Text Types and Purposes

ELA.W.4.1. Write opinion pieces on topics or texts, supporting a point of view with reasons and information.

ELA.W.4.2. Write informative/explanatory texts to examine a topic and convey ideas and information clearly.

ELA.W.4.3. Write narratives to develop real or imagined experiences or events using effective technique, descriptive details, and clear event sequences.

Production and Distribution of Writing

ELA.W.4.4. Produce clear and coherent writing in which the development and organization are appropriate to task, purpose, and audience.

ELA.W.4.5. With guidance and support from peers and adults, develop and strengthen writing as needed by planning, revising, and editing.

ELA.W.4.6. With some guidance and support from adults, use technology, including the Internet, to produce and publish writing as well as to interact and collaborate with others; demonstrate sufficient command of keyboarding skills to type a minimum of one page in a single sitting.

Research to Build and Present Knowledge

ELA.W.4.7. Conduct short research projects that build knowledge through investigation of different aspects of a topic.

ELA.W.4.8. Recall relevant information from experiences or gather relevant information from print and digital sources; take notes and categorize information, and provide a list of sources.

ELA.W.4.9. Draw evidence from literary or informational texts to support analysis, reflection, and research.

Range of Writing

ELA.W.4.10. Write routinely over extended time frames (time for research, reflection, and revision) and shorter time frames (a single sitting or a day or two) for a range of discipline-specific tasks, purposes, and audiences.

Speaking and Listening

Comprehension and Collaboration

ELA.SL.4.1. Engage effectively in a range of collaborative discussions (one-on-one, in groups, and teacher-led) with diverse partners on *grade 4 topics and texts*, building on others' ideas and expressing their own clearly.

Presentation of Knowledge and Ideas

ELA.SL.4.4. Report on a topic or text, tell a story, or recount an experience in an organized manner, using appropriate facts and relevant, descriptive details to support main ideas or themes; speak clearly at an understandable pace.

ELA.SL.4.5. Add audio recordings and visual displays to presentations when appropriate to enhance the development of main ideas or themes.

Introduction:
Nothing Fits in a Box Anymore

This book and the concepts contained within it are a direct response to the growing trend toward differentiation and individualization. The multi-genre, hybrid approach of *Project-Based Writing* recognizes the differences between students, how they learn, and how they seek to show their learning. It caters to their individual strengths, while also guiding them toward the exploration of other means of expression that they might instinctively tend to avoid.

Ultimately, project-based writing is about choice. Just as we live in a culture in which every person in the coffee line can have his or her own personalized beverage made to order, so, too, should students be given the tools and the opportunity to show off their knowledge in many different ways.

A vital aspect of project-based writing is the blending of school life with real life. Often, there is a disconnect between the two. Many students, especially tweens and teens, see school life as totally separate from life outside of school. Therefore, it becomes our job as teachers to make sure that the classroom more directly correlates to the outside world. Choice is a huge part of doing that. So whenever possible in your curriculum, you should feel encouraged to offer student choice, while of course still emphasizing academic rigor and content knowledge.

The multi-genre activities and units covered in *Project-Based Writing* offer the best of both worlds: students gain a functional knowledge of a whole slew of genres, formats, and ways of expressing themselves; and at the same time, they learn to successfully weave these separate elements together into a cohesive whole that digs deeper into the topics, themes, and issues that are most important to their lives outside of school. It is this step of integration that moves students beyond the simple regurgitation of ideas and into a higher level of thinking: that of creation.

How To Use This Book

This book is divided into four parts, each designed to help you, the teacher, guide your students in the creation of project-based writing units.

I. Project-Based Writing and the Multi-Genre Approach (pages 9–12)

Here is where you can find an overview of the ideas behind project-based writing and why the multi-genre approach is so vital to engaging your students and enriching their writing.

II. Creating a Project-Based Writing Unit (pages 13–18)

This section shows you how to begin the process of introducing your students to multi-genre projects. This is where you and your students can start to hone in on the topics and themes that most interest them. It's also where you will learn about the elements that make up each project-based writing unit and where you'll get a glimpse at what a finished product could look like.

III. Resources (pages 19–58)

The resources contained within this section are divided into four main categories:

Activities   **Research**   **Organization**   **Assessment**

Collectively — or in any combination you choose — these resources are intended to provide your students with the tools needed to produce projects that are effective, engaging, and unique. Each page is written to the students, and each is designed to serve as a resource your students can refer back to as they work through the creative process. Each new resource in this section begins with a brief statement explaining how it can be helpful in the creation of a project-based writing unit.

A. Activities

Here you'll find the nuts and bolts of any project-based writing unit. These activities are varied and flexible; they span several genres and skills, and they can be introduced in any order. The aim here is to equip your students with an abundance of options and ideas.

B. Research

This section gives your students practical methods for conducting and recording the research they will need to do in order to dig deeper into their topics.

How To Use This Book *(cont.)*

III. Resources *(cont.)*

C. Organization

Students need to pre-plan and structure their work so that they stay focused and on task. The checklists and multiple outlines provided here will help do just that.

D. Assessment

Need a rubric? There are options for different rubrics in this section, as well as a guide to help your students design their own rubrics. Also included is a form that students can use to record your feedback in their own words.

IV. Pre-Made Project-Based Writing Units (pages 59–96)

Finally, this book includes three pre-made project-based writing units that you can use as is, from beginning to end.

For grade 4, the three pre-made units are as follows:

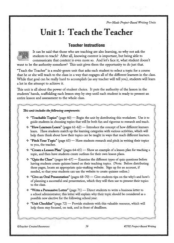

Teach the Teacher

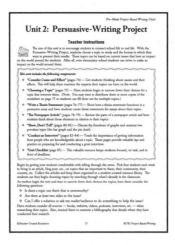

Persuasive-Writing Project

Create a State

Each unit begins with an overview page that provides step-by-step instructions on how to proceed through the unit. You can also dip into the "Activities" section to add or swap out any lesson you wish. It is this ability to interchange lessons and create different combinations of units that makes this concept of project-based writing with a multi-genre emphasis so unique.

What Is Project-Based Writing?

Project-based writing puts a spin on the concept of project-based learning, which is the act of learning through identifying a real-world problem and developing its solution. The project that results from this endeavor encourages students to use critical-thinking skills to journey towards an authentic goal.

Project-based writing activities strive to meet certain criteria. By design, these activities are . . .

❖ multi-genre.

❖ differentiated.

❖ thematic.

❖ both linguistic and non-linguistic.

❖ cross-curricular.

❖ based on real-world scenarios.

❖ guided by student choice.

❖ filled with 21st-century connections.

Project-based writing argues that any subject — be it language arts or STEM — can benefit from strong writing practice. Any genre of writing can support the other. And any engaging activity that links academic learning to the real world can be a 21st-century tool.

10 Reasons to Teach Project-Based Writing

1. It is an organic way to integrate all core subjects — math, science, history, and language arts.

2. It proves to students that imagination and creativity are connected to research and expository writing.

3. It hits all the major elements of the higher levels of Bloom's Taxonomy: Analysis, Evaluation, and Creation.

4. By allowing students to choose their format of showing what they know, the buy-in for the quality of the final project is tremendous.

5. Students develop projects that are individualized, unique, and specific from each other.

6. It is a powerful way to incorporate all multiple intelligences: visual, verbal, logical, musical, physical, social, solitary, and naturalistic.

7. It desegregates nonfiction and fiction, blending the two.

8. It integrates the core subjects with non-core subjects, potentially using technology, art, music, etc.

9. It is a rigorous assessment requiring high levels of thought and communication.

10. It requires use of the entire writing process — from brainstorming to revising, editing, and completing the final draft — regardless of the genres picked and the topic chosen.

The Multi-Genre Approach

At the heart of project-based writing is the concept of melding multiple genres into a final product. This multi-genre approach involves taking several distinct types of writing and fusing them into something unique and powerful. Essentially, a hybrid is created.

Throughout history, humans have strived to create hybrids. In science, people have bred their ideal loyal companion in the Golden Retriever or created their perfect salad accessory in the bug-resistant tomato. In literature, authors and storytellers have written about hybrids, such as the unicorn and Pegasus.

Here are some examples of hybrids throughout history:

Picture	Description
	half electric, half gasoline-powered
	half person, half fish
	half Labrador, half poodle
	half chocolate, half peanut butter

In project-based writing, a hybrid is created when we combine genres that revolve around a shared topic or theme. The result is a multi-genre project that uses the best of different presentations and weaves them together into a totally new creature.

After all, just as any subject can benefit from strong writing practice, so can any genre of writing help support another. The multi-genre aspect of project-based writing is important because it is vital that students understand that genres are not compartmentalized in life. For example, a narrative can support a persuasive argument, just as a graph can support a summary. Weaving the strengths of multiple genres together into one project is the key to project-based writing and to providing one's audience with a richer, fuller picture of a topic or theme.

Differentiation in Education

As you know, there are many different kinds of learners out there in the classrooms. Some students like to write, others like to sing; some like to play sports, while others like to draw. A multi-genre approach allows students to choose ways to show off what they know and what they've learned about a topic, using the methods that are the most interesting to them. Just as importantly, it allows them to challenge themselves and present topics using methods that are not normally in their nature to attempt. So by requiring students to display their content knowledge in multiple ways, you are allowing them to operate within their comfort zones on the one hand, while also pushing them to more fully develop a technique that is challenging to them.

21st-Century Connection: Many students know what interests them, what kind of learner they ar-e, and how they most like to display their knowledge. But it's also very empowering for them to take quizzes that help them identify their natural instincts. With that in mind, consider having students take a test to identify the style in which they learn best. One such four-part quiz is available at The George Lucas Foundation's website, Edutopia.org:

http://www.edutopia.org/multiple-intelligences-learning-styles-quiz

PAGE 1 OF 4

How much time do you spend:

	NONE	ONLY A LITTLE	A FAIR AMOUNT	A LOT	ALL THE TIME
Getting lost in a good book.	○	○	○	○	○
Doing crafts or arts projects.	○	○	○	○	○
Trying to solve mysteries, riddles, or crossword puzzles.	○	○	○	○	○
Writing a journal or blogging.	○	○	○	○	○
Reflecting on your life and your future.	○	○	○	○	○
Playing sports.	○	○	○	○	○
Yearning to spend time with nature.	○	○	○	○	○

(Next Page >)

See page 12 for a complete breakdown of the different types of learners that you may have in your classroom.

Differentiation in Education *(cont.)*

Because we hear so much about differentiation in education, let's take a moment to look more closely at the different ways people learn—and just as importantly for purposes of project-based writing, the different ways people best show what they've learned. This information is usually referred to as "multiple intelligences." Consult the following chart:

The Multiple Intelligences	Some Ways They Learn/Show What They Know
Visual/Spatial	puzzles, maps, 3-D models, charts, graphs, architecture
Verbal/Linguistic	reading, word games, poetry, speeches, lectures
Logical/Mathematical $+ - \times \div$	patterns, puzzles, experiments, investigations, mysteries
Musical/Auditory	songs, lyrics, rhythmic speaking, dance, musical instruments
Physical/Kinesthetic	movement, hands-on activities, acting out, role-playing, realia
Social/Interpersonal	interaction, dialogue, group dynamics, e-mail, video conferencing
Solitary/Intrapersonal	introspection, diaries, journals, books, independent study
Naturalistic	walks; digging; collecting; using microscopes, telescopes, maps, and globes

Choosing a Topic or Theme

The first step a student must take in creating a project-based writing unit is choosing a topic that piques his or her interest. When thinking about a topic, the student might want to choose one with which he or she is somewhat familiar but could learn more about through research. On the other hand, the student could choose a topic he or she has always wanted to know more about but hasn't had the opportunity to explore in detail.

An ideal topic could be anything from a historical event or person to a hot-topic issue that the student wishes to advocate for or argue against.

A theme-based project is another option to consider. Themes, however, can often be discovered and uncovered midway through a topic-based project.

Where to Find Topics

Topics are always out there, ready to be dissected and discussed. Here are just a few of the many possibilities you can present to your students:

❖ **Historical Events or People** — Native Americans • American Revolution • Declaration of Independence • Underground Railroad • Emancipation Proclamation • The Trail of Tears • The Louisiana Purchase • Trojan War • Eruption of Mt. Vesuvius • Abraham Lincoln • Ferdinand Magellan • Julius Caesar • Queen Elizabeth • Susan B. Anthony • Sacagawea

❖ **Writers/Artists/Scientists** — Leonardo Da Vinci • Michelangelo • Donatello • William Shakespeare • Galileo • Copernicus • Lamarck • Kepler

❖ **Recent Events or People** — September 11, 2001 • The Dot-Com Bubble • The Housing Boom and Crash • Bill Gates • Barack Obama • Lance Armstrong • Muhammad Ali • Danica Patrick • Hurricane Katrina • Japan Earthquake and Tsunami of 2011

See page 14 for a great way to create a collaborative classroom resource library!

See page 14 for a great way to create a collaborative classroom resource library!

❖ **Advocacy Issues** — Paying Students for Grades or Attendance • Global Warming • School Budgets • Cloning • Dress Code • Gum Chewing • Cell-Phone Usage • Autism • Eating Disorders

❖ **Themes** — Change • Courage • Acceptance • Loyalty • Success • Aging • Overcoming Adversity

❖ **Morals** — "Beauty is only skin deep." • "Birds of a feather flock together." • "Live and let live." • "Look before you leap."

You may choose to present these to your class, or you could opt for topics that align more closely with your class's curriculum. A list of possible topics could serve as a way to jumpstart your students' thought processes about what kinds of subjects would provide the basis for dynamic project-based writing units.

The Student-Created Resource Library

It's true that you can use the traditional way of having students find their sources, research their topics, and collect their data. But instead, consider making research a collaborative, community-building project for the entire classroom.

Imagine an area of the classroom filled with the resources brought in by the students. As students discover reference material, articles, and chapters from outside the classroom, they bring copies of the material into the classroom and file them in this location for other students to use.

It's easy to start. First, assign a typical advocacy topic that can be found in many different formats. Take, for example, the topic of global warming. Okay, so you've asked students to bring in copies of articles, book pages, etc., all on global warming. Create a file called "Global Warming" and place it in a special file box called "Resource Library." File all of the resources into it.

Try it as a weekly current-events assignment leading up to a research report. It's possible that by the time the students have to actually select a topic, you will have a resource library already underway for that topic.

The great part of this is that it's a growing, dynamic library. As kids settle on their topics, they continue to research and add to the files.

In addition, to encourage further collaboration, keep a chart in the classroom with everyone's names and selected topics so that when students come across research that relates to a peer's topic, they can refer that student to the evidence they found. It's a collaborative form of research that uses the classroom as a working, growing reference library.

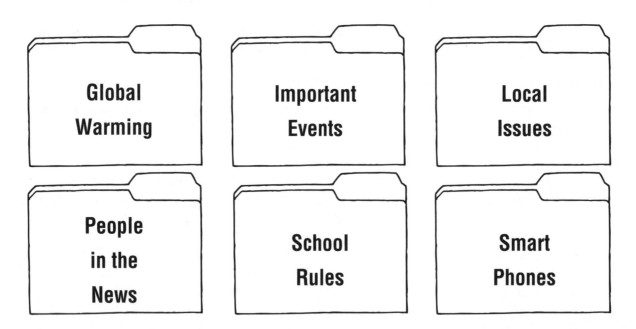

What Are the Parts of a Unit?

In order to create a project-based writing unit, students will use many skills and work in multiple genres. They will do this in all of the steps of the creation process, from planning and research to writing and the production of a final project. This final product will consist of two basic parts: the multi-genre elements and the container.

> *See page 18 for examples of containers and the multi-genre elements they could contain.*

The Multi-Genre Elements

Once students choose the topic or theme on which they will build their projects, they next should begin to think about what elements will make up their final project. These multi-genre elements will comprise the bulk of the project, and they will ideally be a mixture of multiple written and visual genres. In order to really challenge themselves (and also explore more nuances of their topics and themes), students should work not just with the elements with which they are most comfortable. While a visual learner is encouraged to use all of the elements that align with his or her instinctual abilities (say, creating comic books and designing website homepages), that student is also expected to consider penning a persuasive essay or crafting a campaign speech that further illuminates the topic.

A list of possible multi-genre elements is included on the following page. While there is some overlap, the elements are divided into columns depending on whether they are primarily written or visual. You may wish to copy this list and distribute one

> *Many of these elements are explored individually and in greater detail on pages 19–45 of the "Activities" section.*

to each student. Have your students examine each column and circle those activities that they may find interesting to create and that will best illustrate their chosen issue or topic. Also, allow students to add new ideas to the list. As long as the element enriches their project, students should be encouraged to let their imaginations soar.

The Container

One important guiding principle for students to keep in mind is that a project's final appearance will function best if it reflects the theme or subject that it is based on. An appropriate container will go a long way in accomplishing this. Whether it is simple or elaborate, it should function as the final piece that ties all of the other pieces together. Think of the container as the visual delivery system for the project.

A List of Multi-Genre Elements

Directions: Below are lists of possible elements you can combine for use in a project. Examine each column and circle the ones that you may find interesting to create and that will best illustrate your chosen issue or topic. If any other ideas occur to you, record them in the spaces at the bottom of the appropriate column.

Written (Linguistic)	Visual (Non-Linguistic)	Other
Campaign Speech	Advertisement	Directions
Character Sketch	Family Tree	Recipe
Dialogue	Greeting Card	Quiz
Essay	Website	How-to Guide
Fable or Fairy Tale	Picture Book	List
Website	Map	Song
Poetry	Postcard	Dance
Diary Entry	Movie Poster	Board Game
Blog	Diorama	Computer Game
Memoir	Flip Book	Reader's Theater
News Article	Building-Blocks Structure	Podcast
Op-ed Piece	Statue	Video
Petition	Comic Book	Monologue
Advocacy Essay	Comic Life (using iLife suite)	
Letters	Prezi	
Review	PowerPoint	
Script	Blueprint (using Google Sketch-up)	
Glossary		
Narrative		
Interview		
Legend		
Letter of Complaint		
Summary		

Using a Unit Checklist

A checklist is an effective organizational tool that can help students remember what's due and when. There are many different ways to format a checklist. The three pre-made units in this workbook (pages 59–96), for example, contain checklists that are tailored to those projects.

The sample checklist below can give you an idea of appropriate expectations you could have for each student to include in his or her writing unit. For the project below, you may instruct students that the top three assignments must be included. From there, they could be asked to choose one activity from each of the other categories, ensuring that the completed project contains seven pieces in all. This is just one way to approach assigning a unit's components.

Note: A blank checklist is provided on page 54 in the "Resources" section.

Date Due	Date Completed	Assigned Element	Possibilities
		Persuasive Pitch to Teacher About Topic	❖ Letter ❖ Essay
		Research	❖ Cornell Notes ❖ Quickwrites ❖ Movement Survey
		Bibliography/Works Cited	❖ n/a
		Written Piece	❖ Narrative ❖ Poem ❖ Glossary/Dictionary ❖ Interview/Dialogue ❖ Biography ❖ Diary Entry
		Visual or Technological Element	❖ Poster/Ad ❖ Cartoon ❖ PowerPoint/Prezi ❖ Website ❖ Board Game
		Mathematical Piece	❖ Map ❖ Recipe ❖ Step-by-Step Guide
		Musical- or Movement-Based Piece	❖ Cover Song ❖ Original Song ❖ Dance

What Will a Completed Project Look Like?

So what should a completed project-based writing unit look like? The short answer is that there is no one design for how these units should look. In fact, the hope is that each student project looks unique in its display and is specific in its content. Individuality is not only encouraged, it is essential to the concept. Here are some examples:

Project Topic/Theme: Childhood Obesity   **Container/Format:** Pizza Box

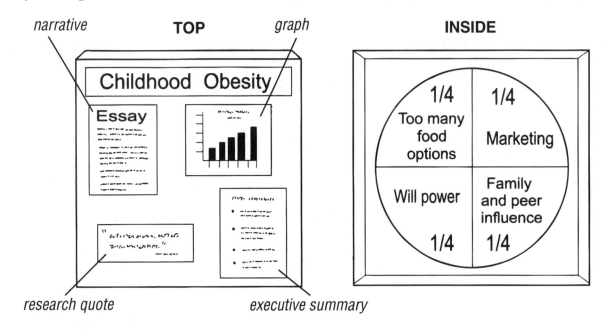

Project Topic/Theme: Pollution   **Container/Format:** Tri-Board Display

Includes: *a research paper on pollution, a science-fiction narrative about a future in which the world has been taken over by trash, comic-book frames illustrating key moments from the narrative, a recipe of the ingredients that make up a dump site, a student-created quiz, the answers to which can be found in the contents of the project*

Playing Think–Tac–Toe

 Project-Based Writing Connection: Use this resource as a brainstorming activity or to help you begin rough drafts for your projects.

Get your creative juices flowing by using these prompts to write about your topic.

Directions: Pick three prompts in a row — either down, across, or diagonally. Follow the directions, and use a separate piece of paper for your responses.

	Narrative	**Response to Literature**	**Persuasive**
Row 1	Write a story in which the main character completely changes.	Find an essay, poem, or piece of art connected to your topic and respond to the author's main message.	Take a stance on your topic and create an ad that displays your stance.
Row 2	Write a story that begins in the middle of an action-packed scene related to your topic.	Find a blog, letter, column, or poem connected to your issue. Rewrite it any way you want. Then write a note explaining what you changed and why.	In a one-page essay, take a stance on your topic and persuade the reader to agree with you.
Row 3	Make up a fairy tale about your topic. Include a moral or lesson at the end.	Find a story, poem, or piece of art connected to your topic and use it to respond to the main character's traits.	Write a persuasive letter to your school principal about your topic.

Getting a Reader's Attention

Project-Based Writing Connection: When adding a written component to your project, use a hook to grab your reader's attention right from the start.

A *hook* is that first moment of a paper — be it a narrative or an essay — that catches the reader's attention and makes him or her want to read more.

Below is a list of hooks using different strategies to begin the same story, a piece called "The First Time I Saw the Ocean." As you can see, there are many ways to hook a reader.

Fact/Statistic	Simile/Metaphor
It was June 28 when I first saw the ocean.	The white crash of the waves looked as soft as cotton, and I felt the spray cooling me like a shower.
In the Middle of the Action	**Definition**
As the wave lifted me off of my feet and tumbled me to the shore, I tried not to laugh out loud.	On a summer day, a beach is a really hot place with a lot of sand and tons of people.
Dialogue	**Onomatopoeia**
"It seems to stretch on forever," I exclaimed in awe. The ocean was so much bigger than I thought it was going to be.	Crash! Sma-bash! The waves slammed into the shore with a loud force.

Directions: After reading each of the examples above, think of an essay you are working on. You may be revising or just beginning. Try to start the piece of writing using each of these strategies. Then, pass your new list of hooks to your classmate or to an adult family member. Have him or her circle the three he or she feels are the strongest. Pick one of these three hooks to use when writing or revising.

Building Better Sentences

Project-Based Writing Connection: By varying sentence length, you can create a rhythm and a flow to your writing.

How can sentences be like roller coasters? Well, some are long and twisting and wrap around, while others are short and fast and dart about. If an entire roller coaster were made up of one kind of experience, it might get boring or predictable. To keep riders on their toes, so to speak, a good roller coaster dips and darts and builds tension. So do great stories and great research papers.

Directions: To learn a little about what it feels like to write long and short sentences and how they add to the texture in an essay, you are going to be asked to complete two strange paragraphs. Both paragraphs will be about pizza. Follow the instructions given in each box to make these two completely different paragraphs about the same topic. Use a separate piece of paper for each.

Paragraph #1	Paragraph #2
Paragraph #1 should be one sentence long. That's all. But this sentence should go on and on. Use this paragraph to write down all of your thoughts on pizza, but do not use punctuation of any kind until you get to the end. This "paragraph" should be at least a half page long.	Paragraph #2 should also be about a half a page long. This paragraph, however, should be made up of many short sentences. These sentences must be full sentences that contain both a subject and a predicate. But, here's the tough part: each sentence can be no longer than five words in length.

Not that you have written both of these paragraphs, use a highlighter to mark the parts of the long sentence that you like. Maybe it's a line or two. Maybe it's just a phrase. Then, use a highlighter and indicate the best short sentences that you've written.

Now it's time to create Paragraph #3. This paragraph should be made up of the best parts of Paragraphs #1 and #2. You must use proper punctuation for this draft. Also be sure to use transition words (*however, therefore, thus,* etc.) to make your paragraph flow smoothly. Write Paragraph #3 on the back of this page or on a separate piece of paper.

Injecting Action Into Verbs

 Project-Based Writing Connection: By replacing dull verbs with more active ones, you can pain a clearer, fuller picture with your words.

When writing a story, it's important to make sure that each word has personality. Each word must help your reader really see the action that is unfolding in your head.

Here's an example of a sentence that does not do that:

❖ Lucy walked to the park.

Can you see *how* Lucy walked to the store? No, but if you use a more specific action verb, the sentence suddenly comes alive:

❖ Lucy ran to the park.   ❖ Lucy skipped to the park.

❖ Lucy shuffled to the park.   ❖ Lucy huffed and puffed to the park.

Directions: In the following activity, cross out each verb that seems a bit boring or ordinary. Then, rewrite the new paragraph. Inject some action-packed action verbs in the places where you have removed the ordinary ones. Make sure your new paragraph still makes sense and has a good flow to it.

Original Paragraph

    Beatrice hit the ball and went toward first base. She ran fast, but the first baseman picked up the ball and stepped on the base. "You're out!" the umpire said. Beatrice slowly walked back to the bench and sat next to her teammates. Paul looked at her, angry. John touched Paul's arm and said, "Hey, it was a good try. You'll get 'em next time, Bea!"

Your New Paragraph

_____

_____

_____

_____

_____

Waking Up Your Words

> **Project-Based Writing Connection:** Use figurative language to liven up your writing and keep your reader interested in what you have to say.

Figurative language is what you use to make your writing wake up and come alive.

You could write a standard, uninspiring sentence like "I waited for the dentist", or, you could put a more original twist on it, for instance . . .

As I waited for the dentist, my hands shook like an earthquake.

There are several different kinds of figurative language you can use to help infuse your writing with interest. There are . . .

❖ **Similes** — These comparisons use *like* or *as*. The above example contains a simile.

❖ **Metaphors** — These are also comparisons, but they don't use *like* or *as*.

   Example: I was a trembling pile of goo waiting for the dentist.

❖ **Hyperboles** — These are crazy exaggerations.

   Example: The whole waiting room could feel the earthquake I was causing with my restless leg.

❖ **Onomatopoeias** — These words are spelled just like they sound.

   Example: Crash! I could just imagine my wildly shaking leg accidentally knocking all the dentist's tools to the floor.

Directions: Give your own examples of figurative language. Use this simple sentence as your inspiration: **I don't like chores.**

1. Rewrite the sentence using a **simile**. _____

   _____

2. Rewrite the sentence using a **metaphor**. _____

   _____

3. Rewrite the sentence using **hyperbole**. _____

   _____

4. Rewrite the sentence using **onomatopoeia**. _____

   _____

Paraphrasing vs. Summarizing

 Project-Based Writing Connection: Paraphrasing and summarizing are vital skills to master; each will help you create unique writing pieces for any project.

Summarizing and *paraphrasing* are two different skills, each with its own purpose. Think of them this way:

❖ **S**ummarizing is **s**horter. You only use the main idea from the piece.

❖ **P**araphrasing **p**uts it into your own words, sentence by sentence.

Directions: In the following activity, you are going to show the differences between summarizing and paraphrasing by using the same paragraph to show an example of both.

On a separate piece of paper, create a dual-entry journal. Title one side "Summarized" and the other "Paraphrased." Use the following paragraph as your informational text:

> Did you know that a city could be built in one day? Perhaps that's an exaggeration, but in 1889, the Oklahoma Land Run helped build a booming town in just a few minutes! It happened at noon on April 22nd. On that day, over 50,000 people had a race to get to free areas of land to claim as their own. In fact, a newspaper from that time printed, "At twelve o'clock on Monday, April 22d, the resident population of Guthrie was nothing; before sundown it was at least ten thousand." In one day, streets were being designed and a town government was being elected. Within two weeks, schools were open. By one month, there were banks and newspapers. The race to win land brought in a lot of people to Oklahoma that day!

Squeezing a Summary

Project-Based Writing Connection: Summarizing helps you persuade a reader, analyze an argument, or move a story along. It's a skill that aids many genres.

Directions: In the following activity, you are going to challenge yourself to squeeze a piece of writing down to its bare essentials. The rules are as follows:

1. The initial paragraph must be stripped down to fit in the space provided below.

2. First cross out information that you feel is too specific to be an important detail.

3. You must use your own words.

4. You must use complete sentences.

Here is the initial paragraph:

> *Florida is known as the "Sunshine State," but it isn't always full of sun. In fact, from 2000 to the present, over 60 hurricanes or cyclones have touched down in Florida. They have caused billions of dollars in damage. Many hurricanes occur from June to November. Residents who live with these natural disasters make sure they listen to the hurricane reports, board up their windows, and stay indoors. Hurricanes may often be a threat, but people still choose to live in the "Sunshine State."*

Now squeeze the key information from the paragraph into this box:

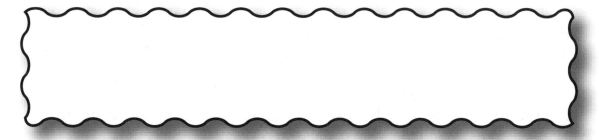

Added Challenge: Take it a step further. Cross out most of the details until only the most essential information remains. Fit what you have left inside this smaller box.

Perfecting the Paragraph

 Project-Based Writing Connection: Effective writing often stems from organization and practice. Use this activity to help you achieve both.

When you are writing a paragraph, you need to make it "sing" — not only that, you want your singing to be in tune, and with perfect pitch. Below is an outline of a pitch-perfect paragraph.

I. Main Topic Sentence — This states what the paragraph is going to be about.

II. Evidence — This states proof about what you've said. It can be in the form of an example, a quote, a statistic, etc.

III. Commentary Sentence(s) — Here is where you put the evidence in your own words and relate it to something else you know.

IV. Concluding Sentence — Here's the place to wrap everything up.

Directions: Below is a paragraph a student has written entitled "Why I Deserve an 'A'." Use this color-coded key to underline or highlight the parts of the paragraph:

❖ Main Topic Sentence = **red**   ❖ Commentary Sentence(s) = **orange**

❖ Evidence Sentence(s) = **yellow**   ❖ Conclusion Sentence = **blue**

> I deserve an "A" because of the effort it took to write my last assignment. I researched different birds in the rainforests, described their habitats, and looked at their declining numbers as humans chop down the trees. I was very specific in my Internet searches. For instance, when I first typed in "rainforests," I received 7,480,000 results. I put more thought into what I was doing, and I made my search more specific. Using an Advanced Search tool, I typed in "birds of the Brazilian rainforests." My results dipped down to 37,000. Of course, I didn't look through all of those, but it became much easier to find what I wanted. I learned a lot about the birds, but I also began to feel for them, too. They are beautiful, and their homes are threatened. In the end, I believe my essay deserves an "A" because my effort can be seen in my paper's quality.

Perfecting the Paragraph *(cont.)*

Teacher Directions: The following activity can show students how to take the parts of a paragraph and assemble them into something that really sings. Begin by making copies of the sentences and cutting them into strips. Then instruct students to mix and match the sentences until they are in the correct order. The result will form a pitch-perfect paragraph about the California Gold Rush.

California was the home of the Gold Rush.

The Gold Rush lasted from around 1848–1855, and during that time experts estimate that over 300,000 people came to find their fortune.

Leaving your family in order to dig for treasure seems so risky today. Would you want to pack up everything you own and travel to a far-off land? You would be doing this with no guarantee of seeing those you love again. It seems like a bad bet on a risky game.

Some did, however. According to pbskids.org, "The work was back-breaking, but flake by flake, nugget by nugget, these lucky forty-niners dug up deposits of gold worth hundreds—or even thousands—of dollars."

Unfortunately, most were not so lucky. Most found nothing but hard work and misfortune.

In the end, the California Gold Rush did not make millionaires out of everyone who migrated there. What it did do, however, was help make California the place it is today.

Mixing in a Moral

 Project-Based Writing Connection: Throughout your project, mix in a moral that sums up your work. This will help hammer home your point.

Have you ever learned a lesson just from reading a story? If so, the author of that story may have intentionally included a moral. A moral is a message. It's like a theme that can sum up the meaning of a story in one, easy-to-remember sentence or phrase.

Here are some morals that you can build a story around. Do they sound familiar to you?

A. It's okay to be different.

B. Never judge a book by its cover.

C. Nothing is permanent, everything changes.

D. Treat others the way you want to be treated.

Directions: Look at each of the project parts described below. Can you match the morals above to each of them? Write the letter of the moral on the line next to the description.

_____ **1.** We may think of mosquitos as small, annoying pests, but they are actually the deadliest animals on Earth! It's true, in many underdeveloped countries, mosquitos are the cause of millions of deaths. Through their tiny bites, they transmit terrible diseases to humans and other animals.

_____ **2.** The drawing on the left shows the quiet, dusty town of San Francisco in 1847, just before the California Gold Rush attracted crowds of people to the area. The picture on the right shows San Francisco today, a bustling city that nearly a million people call home.

_____ **3.** During the Civil War, Dorothea Dix became the head of the North's nursing service. However, Dix and her team of nurses treated wounded soldiers from both the North and the South. She supported the North, but she felt that all wounded soldiers deserved to be helped.

_____ **4.** The platypus is a unique animal that has a bill like a duck, a tail like a beaver, and feet like an otter. It is also the only mammal that can lay eggs.

"Finding" a Poem

 Project-Based Writing Connection: By repeating a key line throughout your project, you can create a found poem that ties the elements together.

A found poem combines your original poetry with a repeating line that is not very poem-like. To create a found poem, you first have to "find" a phrase that you believe really rings true to the heart of your project's topic or theme. You can find lines like that in many unusual places. Here are just a few spots to look:

- ❖ directions
- ❖ recipes
- ❖ horoscopes
- ❖ fortune cookies

- ❖ references
- ❖ ads
- ❖ letters
- ❖ e-mails

- ❖ catalogues
- ❖ textbooks
- ❖ cartoons
- ❖ cereal boxes

For example, let's say you are studying American history and are writing a poem that describes some aspect of the American Revolution. In your search for inspiration, you go into your pantry at home and look at a box of breakfast cereal. The phrase "A Great Way to Wake Up in the Morning" catches your eye. What would a poem based on that phrase look like? How could you tie in that phrase with your historical topic? That's the challenge of creating a found poem.

Directions: Follow each step below to create a found poem.

Step 1: Begin by choosing one of these topics:

- ❖ siblings
- ❖ uniforms

- ❖ scary movies
- ❖ vegetables

- ❖ cell phones
- ❖ helmets

Step 2: You will next need to find a phrase to repeat throughout your poem. Look anywhere in the classroom for your inspiration. Look at the posters on the walls, flip through your textbook, or search through the classroom library. All it takes is one phrase to catch your eye and capture your imagination. Write your phrase here:

_____

Step 3: On a separate piece of paper, write a poem with at least two stanzas. Stay focused on your topic, but also remember to pepper your phrase throughout your poem. By combining these two elements — your topic and your phrase — you can create an interesting and unique final product.

Creating Reading Hybrids

 Project-Based Writing Connection: By fusing elements of two or more genres, you can create a new form of writing to help get your message across.

A *hybrid* combines two different things to form something useful and new. Have you ever heard a song that combined rock and country music, or a dance that was a mix of hip-hop and jazz? These are hybrids that make us perk up our ears (or open up our eyes) and take notice. In the same way, a reading hybrid smooshes two genres into one.

Directions: Complete the form below. After doing so, use the answers you have given to write a short story. Your short story will be a combination of two genres.

Step 1: Begin by choosing two genres from the following list. Circle your choices.

- ❖ Drama
- ❖ Comedy
- ❖ Mystery

- ❖ Mythology
- ❖ Fairy Tales
- ❖ Fantasy

- ❖ Science Fiction
- ❖ Historical Fiction
- ❖ Autobiography

What are two characteristics of Genre #1? _____

_____

What are two characteristics of Genre #2? _____

_____

Step 3: Next, come up with answers to these questions about the story you will be writing. If you need more space, use the back of this paper.

Where is your story set? _____

What is the name of your main character(s)? _____

What do(es) your main character(s) look like? _____

What is the conflict in your story? _____

_____

If there is one, what is the name of the villain/bad guy and what does he or she look like?

_____

What will be the climax (the most exciting part) of the story? _____

_____

Designing a Call to Action

 Project-Based Writing Connection: When stating your position on an issue, it is often necessary to include a solution that makes sense.

One of the most important parts of a persuasive essay is your proposed solution. You have to get your reader to want to do something as a result of learning about your issue.

A "call to action" does that. It calls a group of people together to act on solving a problem. There are many different ways to do this. Here are some methods:

❖ **Debate** — You can have each side present its case in the form of a civil argument.

❖ **Rock-Paper-Scissors** — Have two people compete in a winner-take-all format.

❖ **Compromise** — Each side can give up a little so that a middle ground is reached and everyone "wins."

❖ **Petition** — You can influence an outcome by getting a lot of people to back you up.

❖ **Vote** — You can take a vote, and the majority opinion wins.

Directions: Decide on which method you would like to ask your reader/audience to use in order to solve the problem. Tell why you chose that method.

Statement of Opinion	Call to Action
1. Kids should be able to sit with their friends in class.	Method: _____ Why?: _____ _____
2. There should be a dog park built in the neighborhood.	Method: _____ Why?: _____ _____
3. We need to save our public libraries!	Method: _____ Why?: _____ _____

Conducting a Movement Survey

Project-Based Writing Connection: This activity will help you do research by gauging public opinion about a topic.

In this activity, your class will vote on issues with their bodies by moving to different areas in the classroom. This offers you a quick, visual way of "taking the temperature" of the class on important issues. After conducting the survey, hold a class discussion about the results. This will allow your classmates to explain their choices.

Tip: Conduct the survey twice: once *before* your classmates learn more about the topic (in order to gauge prior knowledge), and once *after* you have presented evidence about the topic (in order to see if their opinions have changed).

For example, imagine that the topic is "dress codes in school." Let's say you are already researching the pros and cons of a school dress code, but you would like to know the opinion of the class before you present any evidence to them.

Here is some language that you can use to conduct a movement survey:

Before you all came into the classroom, I put up two signs: one says "Pro," and the other says "Con." You can see them on either side of the room.

The topic I'm going to be discussing is whether or not schools should have a dress code.

On my signal, you can vote by standing under the sign that matches your opinion.

❖ If you believe that there is a reason that schools should have a dress code, please quietly go stand under the "Pro" sign.

❖ If you believe, without a doubt, that schools should not have a dress code, then go stand under the "Con" sign.

❖ If you are undecided, please go stand in the middle of the two groups in the back of the room.

Directions: Use the form on page 34 to conduct a movement survey in your classroom. Reference the note card provided on page 33 in order to lead a respectful, informative classroom discussion about the results of the survey.

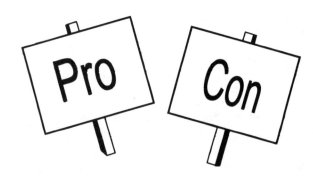

Conducting a Movement Survey *(cont.)*

After conducting the movement survey, you can then lead the class in a discussion about the results. When you permit the participants in the survey to give their rationale for choosing the sides they did, this will provide you with further evidence for your research project. Take notes on what people say, and write down direct quotes whenever possible.

When conducting the discussion part of your survey, it's important to allow one side to talk and the other side to respond *to that point alone*. This is called "refutation," and it is a vital part of a persuasive counterargument. A back-and-forth exchange of dialogue on a key point might look like this:

Student A: A dress code works because it puts us all on an even level of appearance.

Student B: That's an interesting point, and I agree that it evens things out, but it doesn't allow for individuality and diversity in appearance.

Use this note card to keep the discussion respectful and on track:

Here are some guidelines your classmates should keep in mind:

❖ You are agreeing and disagreeing with points, not with people.
❖ If you disagree with a point, that doesn't mean the point isn't important.
❖ People are more likely to listen if you are diplomatic and respectful.

Here are some sentence stems for discussion:

To disagree:
❖ I realize not everyone will agree with me, but . . .
❖ That's an interesting idea, but maybe . . .
❖ I see it a little differently because . . .

To agree:
❖ I agree with what _____ said about . . .
❖ I was wondering/thinking about that, too.
❖ Can I just take that point a step further and say that . . .

To encourage participation:
❖ We haven't heard from you yet.
❖ Could you give me an example of that?

To add to the thought:
❖ May I add something here?
❖ Maybe you could . . .

To clarify:
❖ Could you repeat/rephrase that?
❖ In other words, you think that . . .

Conducting a Movement Survey *(cont.)*

A movement survey is a way for you to conduct a poll by asking people to stand in a place that represents their opinion on a topic.

Step 1:

On the day *before* the activity, write down a little information to read to your pollsters to give them the context of your topic:

❖ Write one sentence that argues **FOR** a side: _____

_____

❖ Write one sentence that argues **AGAINST** that side: _____

_____

❖ Write a question you want to ask your pollsters: _____

_____

Step 2:

On the day of the activity, hang a sign in the room on one wall marked "PRO." Put a sign marked "CON" on the opposite wall. You can decorate your sign with symbols about your topic.

Step 3:

Read your information to your pollsters to give them information on your topic.

Step 4:

Ask students to go stand under the sign that best represents their opinion.

Step 5:

Ask people to give other reasons why they believe the way they do. If you write down the best argument you hear word-for-word, you can use the quote as evidence in your essay.

Number of students who stood under the **PRO** sign: _____

❖ The best argument from the **PRO** side: _____

_____

Number of students who stood under the **CON** sign: _____

❖ The best argument from the **CON** side: _____

_____

Use the information above for your research, advocacy, or persuasive essays.

Reading and Writing a Script

 Project-Based Writing Connection: Use the script format to create characters who are affected by or talking about a topic or theme.

A *script* is a written version of a visually performed medium (a play, a television show, a movie, etc.). It includes the dialogue, a setting, and stage directions.

Here's an excerpt from a script for a sci-fi movie called *Alien in the Bathroom*.

(PETE brushes his teeth in the morning. He looks tired and groggy. Suddenly, a head pops up out of the toilet. PETE screams.)

PETE
Ahhhh! What? Who?

ALIEN
(looking around)
Is it safe to come out now, human? Are the GSA nearby?

PETE
The who? What are you talking about? And what are you doing in my toilet?

ALIEN
I'm hiding from the Galactic Space Authorities. My spaceship crashed in the sewer at the edge of town, and I've been swimming upstream ever since!

(PETE is speechless. He tries to reach for his toothbrush — which he had dropped into the sink — but he's unsuccessful. He can't take his eyes off of ALIEN.)

PETE
(backing away as ALIEN begins to climb out of the toilet)
Whoa. Wait.

ALIEN
(grabbing a towel and drying himself off as if nothing unusual is happening)
Relax, human.

So to write a script takes the following elements:

1. the character names (in all caps)   **3.** the dialogue (no quotation marks)

2. stage directions (in parentheses)

Directions: On a separate sheet of paper, continue the scene by having the two characters exchange some new lines of dialogue. Remember to include the three components — character names, stage directions, and dialogue — formatted properly.

Writing a Recipe for "Success"

 Project-Based Writing Connection: Use the format and elements of recipes to examine a theme or topic in a unique way.

We all know what the average recipe looks like, but have you ever thought of using that format to describe the ingredients of something that you couldn't touch or that wasn't meant to be eaten?

Recipes usually include a few standard elements and often look like this:

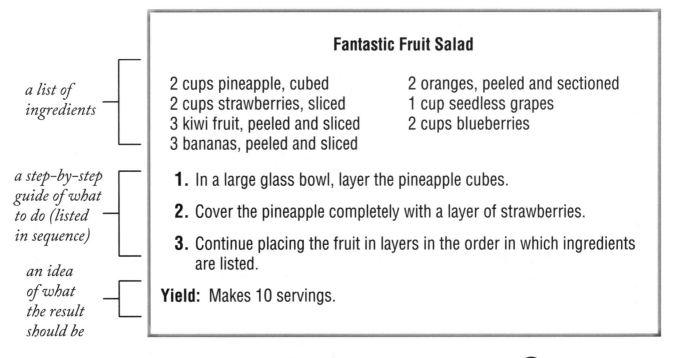

a list of ingredients

Fantastic Fruit Salad

2 cups pineapple, cubed   2 oranges, peeled and sectioned
2 cups strawberries, sliced   1 cup seedless grapes
3 kiwi fruit, peeled and sliced   2 cups blueberries
3 bananas, peeled and sliced

a step-by-step guide of what to do (listed in sequence)

1. In a large glass bowl, layer the pineapple cubes.

2. Cover the pineapple completely with a layer of strawberries.

3. Continue placing the fruit in layers in the order in which ingredients are listed.

an idea of what the result should be

Yield: Makes 10 servings.

What if, instead, you were to use the traditional recipe format to describe what goes into something more abstract, like "imagination" or "success"? You would first need to ask yourself the following questions:

❖ What are the ingredients that make up this abstract idea?

❖ How much of each ingredient is required?

❖ How many will the recipe serve?

❖ What are the stove settings and the cooking times?

Directions: Complete "Cooking Up a Convincing Story" on page 37. Create a recipe for something that can't be eaten or touched. Follow the format shown above.

Cooking Up a Convincing Story

Sometimes it takes planning to get what you want. You have to think of the best way to go about persuading someone to do something for you or give you something. Do it the wrong way, and your hopes will be dashed. But follow the perfect recipe, and your wish might just be granted.

Directions: Imagine that you want something from someone, and all you have to do is come up with the perfect recipe to make it happen. Fill out the form below. What — and how much — will it take?

Sample Idea: "How to Get Your Parents to Buy You a New Video-Game System"

How to _____

Ingredients:

❖ 4 cups of _____

❖ 3 tablespoons of _____

❖ 2 pounds of _____

❖ 1 pinch of _____

Directions for Cooking:

Yield: _____

Using an Illuminated Letter

Project-Based Writing Connection: You can use an illuminated letter to add a visual element to represent your topic in the final draft of a written piece.

An *illuminated letter* is an illustration of a letter, often the first letter of chapter or book. Symbols and icons are drawn into the letter as a way of giving visual hints to the reader. They give the reader an idea about the text that follows.

For instance, let's say that someone was looking at a book of Peter Pan. The first line of that book is as follows:

"All children, except one, grow up."

In this case, the "A" in "All" might look like the letter to the right:

Directions: Look at the illuminated letters below. On the lines next to each, predict the name of the fairy tale in which this letter might appear.

 _____

_____

_____

 _____

_____

_____

Now, let's practice this concept by creating an illuminated letter based on a topic you know a lot about: yourself. Using the first letter of your first name, create a block letter in the space to the right. Then design and fill the rest of the space with symbols that represent you.

Using an Illuminated Border

Project-Based Writing Connection: To visually tie a project together, add a border around the final drafts of your writing.

Much like an illuminated letter, an *illuminated border* can be used to add visual meaning to a written piece. However, by using the margins of a document, an illuminated border frames the text. It creates a decorative picture around the page. This allows the artist to depict not only symbols, but also landscapes or scenes, much in the same way a comic-book artist of today will sequence a story.

Remember, the illuminated border always stays focused on the main idea of the text.

Directions: Look at the page below. Inside the page, there is a paragraph about growing tomatoes. In the framed border surrounding the paragraph, create an illuminated border that captures the main idea of the paragraph.

Do you like tomatoes on your hamburger, on your pizza, or in your salad? Well, growing your own tomatoes is easy to do. The first-time grower should buy small tomato plants at a nursery, but once you've grown them a few seasons, it's easy to grow them from seeds. All you need to grow your perfect, juicy tomatoes is a lot of sun, a good amount of water, and some deep, rich dirt. Keep your eye on them and watch them change from green to red in just a couple of months. Fresh tomatoes are yours if you have the patience and the desire!

Creating a Comic Strip

 Project-Based Writing Connection: Use the format of a comic strip (brief text, illustrations) to highlight the important points in a narrative.

You have probably read (and enjoyed) a comic strip before. But did you realize that a comic strip is a perfect multi-genre project? After all, it combines pictures and writing.

Begin this next activity by reading the following poem:

My Shadow
by Robert Louis Stevenson

I have a little shadow that goes in and out with me,
And what can be the use of him is more than I can see.
He is very, very like me from the heels up to the head;
And I see him jump before me, when I jump into my bed.

The funniest thing about him is the way he likes to grow—
Not at all like proper children, which is always very slow;
For he sometimes shoots up taller like an india-rubber ball,
And he sometimes gets so little that there's none of him at all.

He hasn't got a notion of how children ought to play,
And can only make a fool of me in every sort of way.
He stays so close beside me, he's a coward you can see;
I'd think shame to stick to nursie as that shadow sticks to me!

One morning, very early, before the sun was up,
I rose and found the shining dew on every buttercup;
But my lazy little shadow, like an arrant sleepy-head,
Had stayed at home behind me and was fast asleep in bed.

Directions: Begin this assignment by highlighting the three most interesting or important lines in the poem. Then, on a separate piece of paper, draw these moments. Imagine that you are zooming in on one important detail for each moment.

Creating a Comic Strip *(cont.)*

Directions: Use the frames below to create a comic strip based on your topic. First, you have to decide what are the most important elements of the story or argument to draw. Then, you have to decide on the visual style of your drawing.

Here is a list of elements to focus on:

Story Elements	Writing Devices	Camera Angles

❖ plot
❖ setting
❖ characters
❖ descriptions
❖ conflict
❖ resolution
❖ theme
	❖ hook
	❖ sequence
	❖ suspense
	❖ foreshadowing
	❖ zooming in
	   on a moment
	❖ dialogue
		❖ close-ups
		❖ ¾ shots
		❖ long shots
		❖ foreground vs.
		   background

Making a Flip Book

Project-Based Writing Connection: A flip book is a great way to show — both textually and visually — a sequence of steps or events.

A flip book is a mini project in itself that includes both writing and art in order to describe a sequence of steps or events. These steps can form a how-to description, a summary of a novel, a chronological timeline, or even a scientific guide through a particular process. The different pages of the flip book can also be used to illustrate the different elements of a complex issue.

In order to make a flip book, you need these materials:

- ❖ several sheets of paper
- ❖ stapler
- ❖ drawing supplies
- ❖ pen

Then, follow these steps:

1. Stagger several sheets of paper in order to create visible tabs.

2. Next, fold the sheets to create a booklet of consistently spaced tabs.

3. Staple the booklet's folded edge.

4. On the cover, give your flip book a title (the name of the book, the name of the process being described, etc.). Also write your name.

5. Label the tabs by section or chapter.

6. Fill in your summaries, responses, and art.

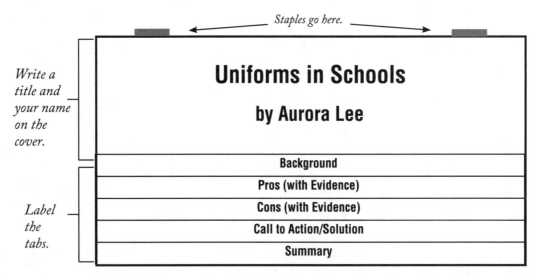

Staples go here.

Write a title and your name on the cover.

Uniforms in Schools

by Aurora Lee

Label the tabs.

| Background |
| Pros (with Evidence) |
| Cons (with Evidence) |
| Call to Action/Solution |
| Summary |

Creating a Homepage

 Project-Based Writing Connection: You can use the format of a website's homepage to showcase many different projects related to the same topic or theme.

When it comes to websites, there's no place like the *homepage*. A good homepage includes a variety of information and formats, and it invites and entices users to visit the rest of the other content on the site.

A homepage has many elements, and they should be laid out in a way that is informative and clear to read. Here are two elements usually found on homepages:

❖ **Banner** — The banner runs along the top of the homepage. It often includes a title, a slogan, and a visual that represents the company/person who runs the website.

❖ **Menu Bar** — Often located in the banner, the menu bar lists the main categories that make up the website. These are links that the user can click on to visit those pages/sections of the site (for example, "Home," "Blog," "About," "Resources").

Directions: In the space below, sketch a rough draft of a homepage for a website about your chosen topic. Include a banner and a menu bar. Below the banner, include text, pictures, and links that would entice visitors to want to read and see more of what is on the other pages of your website.

21st-Century Connection: With parents' or teacher's permission, you can go online and create a website using something like *www.wordpress.com* or *www.edublogs.org*.

Using Technology to Present

 Project-Based Writing Connection: Add extra appeal by using a 21st-century, technology-based method to present your project.

These days, we don't just explain what we know through oral presentations or the traditional book report; we use technology to display and communicate our knowledge.

Think about what you would want to watch or listen to or read, and then go ahead and create that for your work. Listed below are three possible ways you can display what you've learned in a method that reflects the age you live in, the Age of Technology:

❖ **Set Up a Screencast** — Using an iPad app like Educreator or ShowMe, you can display an image and record narration. You can then submit it from your tablet directly to the website. A link will be provided, which you can submit to your teacher for viewing.

Example: Let's say your project involves designing your own country. Open up a screencasting app and draw the map of your country. Include borders, the most important cities, and symbols to represent geographical features. Narrate as you draw so that your viewers can hear your description of the country.

❖ **Produce a Prezi** — A Prezi uses a concept map rather than slides to go from idea to idea. What's unique about a Prezi is that you can load an image that represents your whole topic and then "zoom in" on the details that show off your knowledge on that topic. If you go to *http://prezi.com*, you can see examples of this cool presentation software. You can create your presentation for free, and it's stored on the web, always there for your teacher to access it.

Example: If your project is about saving an endangered species, you can upload an image of the animal and zoom in on specific features.

❖ **Make a Movie** — There are so many ways to create a digital movie. Whether you are using iMovie on a Mac or producing a free, web-based, 30-second movie using Animoto, you have options.

Example: find visuals to represent each step of your project. Upload them into Animoto, add some copyright-free music from a site like *www.Soundzabound.com*, and watch a 30-second narrative of your work in pictures and music. Send the link to your teacher.

Directions: Let's say your subject is texting while on the move (walking, riding a bicycle, riding a skateboard, etc.). Think about your position on this activity. Then think about which of the above methods would be the best way to give a presentation on this subject. Give a complete answer on a separate piece of paper.

Wrapping It All Up

 Project-Based Writing Connection: A container provides an attractive way to present your final project and tie all of its individual elements together.

Finding a visual way to present your project is important when getting ready to turn in the final results. The package or container in which you house your work is another opportunity to show what you know. It's like the punctuation at the end of the sentence or the glue that holds it all together. It's a visual way to really send home your message with your audience.

Directions: In the activity below, draw lines to match the container with its appropriate topic. The first one has been done for you.

Pizza Box with essays inserted inside	**Pollution**
Clothes Hanger with essays dangling below at different levels	**Body Image**
Mailbox with a collage of essays taped onto its surface	**Childhood Obesity**
Rolled Scrolls tied together with a ribbon and quill	**Getting Rid of the Post Office**
Trash-Can Lid with essays glued to the inside	**The History of the Amendments**

Now, what containers would you pick for the following topics?

1. Protecting endangered species _____

2. Global warming _____

3. Library closures _____

Ask Yourself: What container could you use to house your own project? How would that container help your audience connect with your topic?

Cornell Notes

Project-Based Writing Connection: This resource can help you organize and process information for any project.

Cornell notes are a great way to organize your researched information. A page of Cornell notes is divided into three main sections:

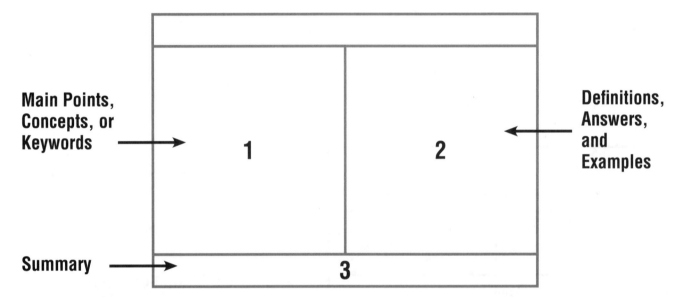

Here is a brief description of those sections:

1. **Main Points, Concepts, or Keywords** — Record this information in the left-hand column on the page. Main ideas and key elements (dates, people, etc.) should be included here. Also use this space to develop questions that need to be answered about the topic.

2. **Definitions, Answers, and Examples** — This information should be recorded in the right-hand column. Use this space to explain the terms and answer the questions listed on the left. Be brief and clear. Use bullets or short phrases and skip lines between ideas.

3. **Summary** — A brief statement of the topic and your finding should be recorded here. Aim to summarize the information in three sentences or less.

Reminder: Don't forget to put such information as your name, the date, and your topic along the top of your page of Cornell notes.

You can use these instructions to create your own Cornell notes on a piece of lined paper, or you can use the blank template provided on page 47.

Cornell Notes *(cont.)*

Directions: Use this template to help organize your research about your topic.

Name:	Date:
Topic:	**Class:**

Main Points, Concepts, or Keywords:	**Definitions, Answers, and Examples:**

Summary:

Bibliographies

Project-Based Writing Connection: This resource shows you how to cite the information used in research projects. (Blank forms are on page 49.)

Every research essay needs evidence, and every piece of evidence came from somewhere. It's important, therefore, to learn how to create a proper bibliography.

Bibliography Cheat Sheet

Book

Author's last name, first name. *Book title.* City of publication: Publishing company, Publication date. Pages. Medium.

Example:

Blume, Judy. *Superfudge.* New York: Dutton Children's Books. 12–23. Print.

Article in a Newspaper or Magazine

Author's last name, first name. "Article title." *Periodical title.* Month, Year: Pages of actual article. Medium.

Example:

Smith, John. "Dancing with the Cars." *Car and Driver Monthly.* April, 2003: 12–14. Print.

Website

Author. Date. "Name of article." *Name of website.* Date retrieved and where retrieved (URL).

Example:

Delbanco, Andrea. May 6, 2011. "A Modern Fairy Tale. *Timeforkids.com.* Retrieved on July 5, 2011 from *http://www.timeforkids.com/.*

Interview

Subject's last name, first name. Personal Interview. Date of interview (day, month, year).

Example:

Spielberg, Steven. Personal Interview. 14 January 2011.

Movie

Title. Name of director. Year of release. Format. Studio, release date of format.

Example:

E.T: The Extraterrestrial. Steven Spielberg. 1982. DVD. Universal Studios, 2005.

21st-Century Connection: The website *www.easybib.com* offers a free way to create bibliography entries. Just type in the information, and it puts it into the correct format.

Bibliographies *(cont.)*

Directions: Use these forms to record information as you gather research. You may not be able to fill in every line, depending on the information provided.

Information Source: Book

Author's Name: _____

Title of Book or Selection: _____

Series Title: _____

Editor or Translator's Name: _____

Edition and Volume Number: _____

Publisher: _____

Publication City and Date: _____

Page Numbers: _____

Information Source: Periodical (magazine, newspaper, etc.)

Author's Name: _____

Title of Article: _____

Title of Periodical: _____

Series and Volume Numbers: _____

Publication Date: _____

Page Numbers: _____

Information Source: Internet

Author's Name: _____

Title of Article or Page: _____

Name of Website or Company: _____

URL: _____

Publication Date (or Date Last Revised): _____

Access Date: _____

Outlines

Project-Based Writing Connection: The resources on pages 50–52 can help you get organized before you begin writing an essay.

The outline on this page focuses on helping you write a narrative, or story.

A **narrative/story** is a piece of writing or speech that describes a sequence of events. A narrative can be completely fictional (like a fantasy) or based on truth to some degree. It includes any kind of story—from science fiction to love stories to personal memoirs.

Here are some elements to look for when reading and revising narratives:

I. The Opening (Exposition)
- **A.** Hook
- **B.** Characters
   - **1.** Physical Traits
   - **2.** Personality Traits
- **C.** Setting
- **D.** Main Story Conflict

II. The Body (Rising Action — Climax — Falling Action)
- **A.** Sequential Events (or flashback if using that strategy)
- **B.** Sensory or Emotion Details (sight, smell, touch, taste, sound, feel in your heart)
- **C.** Foreshadowing/Suspense
- **D.** Figurative Language (simile, metaphor, onomatopoeia, personification, etc.)
- **E.** Dialogue
- **F.** Description of Facial Expression, Gestures
- **G.** Transitions
- **H.** Action Verbs

III. The Ending (Resolution)
- **A.** "Tie it all up"
- **B.** Lesson Learned, Theme, Moral, Motto, etc.

Hint! Remember to incorporate these six traits of good writing for added sophistication:

- ❏ Sentence Variety
- ❏ Voice
- ❏ Proper Conventions
- ❏ Word Choice
- ❏ Great Ideas
- ❏ Organization

Outlines

The outline on this page focuses on helping you craft a **persuasive essay**. This type of writing is meant to influence and change minds. Being able to write a successful persuasive essay is an important skill. Use the strongest word choices and evidence in order to increase your chances of convincing your readers.

Here are some elements to look for when reading and revising persuasive writing:

I. Introduction
  A. Hook
  B. Background Information
  C. Who is affected by this issue?
  D. Thesis Statement (Opinion + Reason #1 + Reason #2)
     For instance: *I strongly believe that the school vending machines should only sell water because it is a healthy alternative to sugary drinks and it costs less to buy.*

II. Body paragraph: Reason #1
  A. Main Topic Sentence (general statement)
  B. Expansion of the Main Topic (gets more specific)
  C. Textual Evidence/Proof (quotes, statistics, data, personal experience, etc.)
  D. Commentary/Connection to the evidence
  E. Transition to next paragraph

III. Body paragraph: Reason #2
  A. Main Topic Sentence (general statement)
  B. Expansion of the Main Topic (gets more specific)
  C. Textual Evidence/Proof (quotes, statistics, data, personal experience, etc.)
  D. Commentary/Connection to the evidence
  E. Transition to next paragraph

IV. Counterargument
  A. Main Topic Sentence (states the opposing side's *best* point)
  B. Expansion of the Main Topic (gets more specific)
  C. Textual Evidence/Proof (quotes, statistics, data, personal experience, etc.)
  D. Commentary/Connection to the evidence
  E. Conclusion that *refutes* this point (i.e., why it doesn't convince you)

V. Conclusion
  A. Restate Thesis (using different words)
  B. Solution/Call to Action (what we should do about it)

Outlines *(cont.)*

The outlines on this page focus on two different types of essays, the summary and the reading-response.

A **summary** is a brief overview of a piece of writing. It gives a reader the most important points. The key in writing a summary is to make it simple so that it is easily understood.

An outline of a summary might look like this:

I. Main Topic Sentence

    A. Include the writing's title, author, and genre.

    B. Keep this sentence general.

II. Most Ideas

    A. Only use the most important points.

    B. Don't use small details.

    C. Use transitions.

    D. Go in chronological (time) order.

    E. Don't use voice.

    F. Use sentence variety.

III. Conclusion

    A. Quickly restate main point.

    B. Don't give your opinion.

A **reading-response** essay gives you a chance to write about something you have read. You might use such an essay to explain your personal feelings about a book or to give your thoughts about what the author was trying to say.

An outline of a reading-response essay might look like this:

I. Introduction

    A. Hook

    B. Background information

    C. Main topic sentence

II. Body Paragraphs

    A. Reasons supporting your main topic sentence

    B. Quotations that illustrate your reasons

    C. Explanations of what the quotations mean and how they support your point

    D. Graceful transitions

III. Conclusion

    A. Main topic sentence restated and explained

    B. Parting thoughts

The Writing-Genre Chart

 Project-Based Writing Connection: This resource can get you thinking about different forms of writing.

Directions: Study the chart below, which shows the various elements that go into five different genres of writing: Narrative, Summary, Argument (Persuasive), Response to Literature, and Informational.

Teacher Note: This chart is meant to get students thinking about the overlap in writing genres. The categorization of these elements may be up for debate. For instance, it could be said that "voice" can be found in many genres. Use this resource to spark a classroom discussion about writing.

Genre	Narrative	Summary	Argument	Response	Informational
Hook	√		√	√	
Background Info	√		√	√	√
Thesis Statement			√	√	√
TAG (title/author/genre)		√		√	
Main Topic Sentence		√	√	√	√
Evidence			√	√	√
Commentary			√	√	√
Transition Words	√	√	√	√	√
Voice	√				
Sentence Variety	√	√	√	√	√
Conventions	√	√	√	√	√
Figurative Language	√				
Plot	√				
Setting	√				
Characters	√				
Conflict	√		√		
Theme	√	√			
Counterarguments			√		
Call to Action/Solution			√		

Unit Checklist

Project-Based Writing Connection: A checklist can help you organize your time and your work so that you never lose sight of your deadlines.

Here are some tips for using this checklist.

❖ In the "Assigned Element" column, fill in a more general type of element, like "Research" or "Written Piece" or "Visual Element."

❖ Use the "Possibilities" column to think of ways you could meet those requirements, like "Survey" for research or "Movie Poster" for visual element. Try to jot down a lot of ideas in the "Possibilities" column.

Date Due	Date Done	Assigned Element	Possibilities

Using Rubrics

 Project-Based Writing Connection: Rubrics can help you understand what is expected of you before you begin each element of a project.

Rubrics serve two important purposes:

1. Rubrics tell a student how he or she did.
2. By clearly defining your expectations to students, rubrics serve as preemptive feedback.

Over the next few pages, several rubrics are featured. They fall into two categories:

> **teacher-created**

> **student-created**

Both can be used peer-to-peer to evaluate student rough drafts, or they can be used to evaluate a final project itself.

If completed prior to producing the actual project, a student-created rubric can really motivate students by driving home what is necessary to achieve the highest score possible.

Before handing out the student-created rubric worksheet on page 57, distribute copies of the card below to students. It can serve as a step-by-step "How To" guide for students to follow as they create their rubrics.

Creating a Rubric

Creating a rubric for an element of a project (a narrative, an oral presentation, an expository paper, visual, etc.) is simple. It just takes three basic steps:

Step 1: In the left-hand column, list the qualities that you believe are the most important in order to do well on the project.

Step 2: Across the top, list the rankings that would describe how well a person did. Do this by writing a number and a word. For instance, you could write a "4 – Fantastic" in the first box, and you could write "1 – Poor" in the last box.

Step 3: In the boxes of the matrix, write descriptions of what the various scores would look like. Use words that you know.

Using Rubrics *(cont.)*

Teacher-Created Rubrics

Below are different possible rubric templates that can be used with various projects.

Project Rubric

Criteria	Exceeds	Meets	Approaching	Not Evident
Research Quality				
Theme Appears Throughout				
Quality of Writing				
Creativity				
Neatness				
Organization				
Bibliography				
Conventions				
Presentation				

Oral-Presentation Rubric

Criteria	3	2	1
Volume			
Stance			
Eye Contact			
Information Quality			
Intonation			
Speed			

Using Rubrics *(cont.)*

Student-Created Rubrics

A rubric helps a teacher score your projects and essays. Rubrics go beyond just giving a letter or number grade. They explain what it is that you need to do to earn a high score (or improve a low score). A great way to understand rubrics is by creating one.

Directions: Look at the rubric below. Along the left-hand side, it lists some categories. These categories are some of the things that make up strong, effective writing. Think about what it takes to get the highest grade possible in each of those categories. Also, think of what it would take to get the next highest grade, and so on. The first category has been filled in for you to give you an idea of how rubrics work.

	4 (Awesome!)	3	2	1
Word Choice	My words are the best options. I use great synonyms, and I think hard about what is the best word for the job.	I thought about my words, but they may not have always been the best. They are at my grade level, but I didn't push myself more than that.	My words are simple and to the point, with no creative choices.	I repeat a lot. My words are definitely below my grade level.
Sentence Fluency				
Organization				
Ideas				

Teacher Feedback

 Project-Based Writing Connection: Get one-on-one time with the teacher to help you focus on what you are doing right and what you need to work on.

At times, you might need help with some part of your project. Often, a quick meeting with your teacher will do just the trick. Be prepared to make the most out of the opportunity to receive such helpful feedback. Use the form below to take notes during your meeting. You can use these notes later as a reference when you are revising or finalizing your paper.

Own Your Own Feedback

Notes on Your Topic/Theme: _____

_____

_____

Notes on Your Thesis Statement: _____

_____

_____

This is great: Keep doing it, don't change a thing! (List skills you've done well.)

_____

_____

This could be better: Reconsider and revise. (List items you still need to work on.)

_____

_____

Based on the work in front of me today, my teacher is giving me a(n) _____.

(enter grade)

Think about it: Am I satisfied with that grade?   Yes   No

Due date of final draft, based on our discussion: _____

Signed: _____   Date: _____

Unit 1: Teach the Teacher

Teacher Instructions

It can be said that those who are teaching are also learning, so why not ask the students to teach? After all, knowing content is important, but being able to communicate that content is even more so. And let's face it, what student doesn't want to be the authority somehow? This unit gives them the opportunity to do just that.

"Teach the Teacher" is a multi-genre unit that asks each student to select a topic for a course that he or she will teach to the class in a way that engages all of the different learners in the class. While that goal can be really hard to accomplish (as any teacher will tell you), students will learn a lot in the attempt to achieve it.

This unit is all about the power of student choice. It puts the authority of the lesson in the students' hands, scaffolding each lesson step by step until each student is ready to present an entire lesson and assessment to the whole class.

This unit includes the following components:

- ❖ **"Teachable Topics"** (page 60) — Begin the unit by distributing this worksheet. Use it to guide students in choosing topics that will be both fun and rigorous to research and teach.

- ❖ **"How Learners Learn"** (pages 61–62) — Introduce the concept of how different learners learn. Have students match up the learning categories with various activities, which will help them think about how their topics can be taught in ways that reach different learners.

- ❖ **"Pitch Your Topic"** (page 63) — Have students research and pitch in writing their topics to you, the teacher.

- ❖ **"Create a Lesson Plan"** (pages 64–65) — Show an example of a lesson plan for teaching a topic, and then have students create outlines for their own lesson plans.

- ❖ **"Quiz the Class"** (pages 66–67) — Examine the different types of quiz questions before having students create quizzes based on their teaching topics. (Note: Before distributing these pages, locate an appropriate quiz-making website. Sign up for an account, if needed, so that your students can use the website to create quizzes online.)

- ❖ **"Give an Oral Presentation"** (pages 68–70) — Give students tips on the why's and how's of planning a successful oral presentation, which they will then use to present their topics to the class.

- ❖ **"Write a Persuasive Letter"** (page 71) — Direct students to write a business letter to a school administrator; this letter will explain why their topic should be considered as a possible new elective for the following school year.

- ❖ **"Unit Checklist"** (page 72) — Provide students with this valuable resource, which will help them stay focused, on task, and in front of deadlines.

Teachable Topics

At last, the time has come for you to teach the teacher (and all of the other students in your class). Has there ever been a topic that has made you think, "Why don't they teach that in school?" Now you will get the chance to not only teach this topic, but also to persuade your teacher and your school that this topic should be taught every year.

The question remains: What will you choose to teach everyone about? Your topic can be anything from "The History of . . ." (basketball, blue jeans, smart phones, etc.) to "How to . . ." (prepare a healthy meal, throw a curveball, master a particular video game, etc.). The possibilities are endless.

Choose a topic with which you are familiar but about which you can learn more through research. After all, the more knowledge you can bring to this topic, the better chance you will have to show everyone that it is a subject worth studying.

Directions: Think of two possible topics for you to teach. List the pros and cons of teaching each topic. "Pros" may be how much you know about the topic, how interesting you think it will be for others to learn, etc. "Cons" may be that it would be difficult for others to learn, the cost or availability of materials needed to teach the class, etc.

Possible Topic #1 _____

   Pros: _____ Cons: _____

         _____   _____

         _____   _____

Possible Topic #2 _____

   Pros: _____ Cons: _____

         _____   _____

         _____   _____

Now look back at your two possible topics. It's time to make your choice.

                My Choice →

How Learners Learn

A good teacher wants to know how his or her students learn. This will help him or her design lessons that are interesting to lots of students.

Take a look at the seven categories listed here. They describe the different ways in which people learn. You may not fit into just one category; you may learn in several different ways. But knowing these seven learning styles can help you create a lesson that will appeal to many different students.

Learning Style	How the Learner Learns
Interpersonal	learns best through a deep understanding of oneself; thinks deeply
Kinesthetic	learns best through sports and movement
Linguistic	learns best through language (words, writing)
Logical	learns best through science and math (numbers, charts, and graphics)
Musical	learns best through tone, rhythm, and dance
Natural	learns best through an understanding of nature and the world outside
Visual	learns best through art, design, and shapes

Directions: In the boxes below, create symbols or drawings to represent each category. For example, you may draw an old-fashioned pen to represent Linguistic.

Interpersonal

Kinesthetic

Linguistic

Logical

Musical

Natural

Visual

Now use the symbols you drew to complete the activity on the next page.

How Learners Learn *(cont.)*

Look at the examples of activities below. Match the kind of learning to the activity. Do this by drawing in the box the symbol you created on the previous page. If you think more than one kind of learning applies, draw multiple symbols.

As the teacher, you ask your students to . . .

1. design a poster to advertise for your topic. **Symbol(s):**	**5.** write a diary entry from the point of view of an historical figure associated with your topic. **Symbol(s):**
2. write an original song about a topic. **Symbol(s):**	**6.** write a journal entry about how your topic may have come to be a part of our world in the first place. **Symbol(s):**
3. play charades in small groups to act out vocabulary. **Symbol(s):**	**7.** give a short speech about how the topic can apply to their lives outside of school. **Symbol(s):**
4. create a timeline of events in the history of your topic. **Symbol(s):**	**8.** create and perform a dance that illustrates the topic. **Symbol(s):**

- -

Teacher Note: Fold this section under to cover it before making copies.

Possible answers: **1.** visual; **2.** musical; **3.** kinesthetic; **4.** logical; **5.** linguistic; **6.** linguistic, natural; **7.** interpersonal; **8.** musical, kinesthetic

Pitch Your Topic

Have you ever wanted to teach your classmates something they never knew before? Well, in the "Teach the Teacher" project, you are going to be given the chance to do just that! But first, you have to get your idea approved by your teacher. You will do this by pitching — making the case for — your project.

Directions: Use this form to help you convince your teacher that your topic is worthy of being taught. Use the results to write a persuasive paragraph on a separate piece of paper.

I. Hook — Begin your essay with a sentence that will grab your teacher's attention.

_____

_____

II. Background Information — Pretend your teacher knows nothing about this topic. Write one or two sentences to give him or her some background on the subject.

_____

_____

III. Thesis Statement — Try to write one sophisticated statement that says what you want to study and why. Use the following format:

I want to be permitted to research _____ *because* _____.

Give two reasons why this topic is fascinating to you.

_____

_____

_____

IV. Counterargument — Give a one-sentence counterargument that acknowledges why your teacher might be skeptical of allowing you to spend time researching your topic.

_____

_____

V. Your Response — Write one sentence that speaks directly to your teacher's concerns, and convince him or her why you should still be permitted to continue with your subject.

_____

_____

Create a Lesson Plan

In order to engage learners, you need a plan. Many teachers design formal lessons plans for each lesson in order to break down how to best communicate their content to the class. You will now create a plan that includes these elements:

❖ **Objective** — What is the specific skill that you want your class to know? What is the broader lesson that you will be teaching?

❖ **Materials** — List the things you will need to conduct your lesson. This is not only for you, but also for your teacher so he or she can provide you with the items.

❖ **Step-by-Step Lesson** — Give some thought to what you will do first, second, third, etc., as you walk through the lesson.

❖ **Check for Understanding** — Develop some questions to ask students as you progress through your lesson to make sure that the students are "with you."

❖ **Assessment** — Create and distribute a quiz to assess how well your students listened, as well as how effectively you presented your material.

Here is a sample lesson plan that follows this outline:

Objective: I want my class to learn about the history of toasters.

Materials:

❖ toaster ❖ poster ❖ computer

❖ PowerPoint ❖ bread ❖ LCD projector

Step-by-Step Lesson:

Step 1: Introduce materials.

Step 2: Talk about how people used to toast bread before toasters were invented. Give name of inventor. Use PowerPoint presentation to explain how first toasters operated. Show how they evolved into the options we have now.

Step 3: Toast bread.

Step 4: Describe what's happening as the bread toasts. Explain how the toaster does it.

Check for Understanding:

1. Ask, "What else do you use toasters for?"

2. Ask review question: "Who invented the toaster?"

3. Ask, "Could someone share with us what kind of toaster he or she has at home?"

Assessment: Distribute a 5-question quiz to students.

Create a Lesson Plan *(cont.)*

It is your turn to create a lesson plan that will help you teach your topic to the class.

Directions: Follow the outline below to create a rough draft of your lesson plan.

Objective: _____

_____

Materials:

Step-by-Step Lesson (only fill in as many steps as are needed):

Step 1: _____

Step 2: _____

Step 3: _____

Step 4: _____

Step 5: _____

Step 6: _____

Step 7: _____

Check for Understanding:

1. _____

2. _____

3. _____

Assessment: _____

Quiz the Class

Have you ever wanted to develop your own quiz? Now is your chance. And as an added bonus, you might find that by designing questions for your classmates to answer, you will learn even more about topic.

You are going to develop a 5-question quiz on your topic. In order to do this, let's first look at the different types of questions that make up quizzes.

> Here are three different kinds of questions to include in your quizzes:
>
> ❖ A **forced-choice** question is one that "forces" the test-takers to settle on an answer that the test-creator previously determined.
>
>   *Examples of forced-choice questions:* Multiple Choice, True/False, Matching
>
> ❖ A **rank-order** question is one that asks an opinion of the test-taker, but it still must be given within a set range.
>
>   *Examples of rank-order questions:* Star Rating ("1 star" for worst, "5 stars" for best), Assigning a Letter Grade ("A" for best, "B" for next best, etc.)
>
> ❖ An **open-ended** question is one that gives the authority to the test-taker, allowing him or her to determine the answer.
>
>   *Examples of open-ended questions:* Short Answer, Essay Response

Directions: On a separate piece of paper, create your own quiz based on your lesson presentation. It should be made up of the following types of questions:

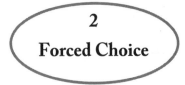

When you are creating your own quiz, you should take inspiration from the assessments you've taken as a student. Which kinds of question do you believe really challenge you to remember the material? Which kinds of question are the most engaging?

21st-Century Connection: Go online to a quiz-making website that your teacher has chosen. There, you can design a quiz using the different methods above. Have your classmates take the test, and the website will score and assess the results.

Quiz the Class *(cont.)*

In the following activity, look at the questions and decide if they are **Forced Choice**, **Rank Order**, or **Open-Ended**. Then, explain why you believe the way you do. The first one has been done for you.

Hint: Only answer the "What type of question is it?" and the "Why?" questions.

Question #1. Should vending machines with soda and candy be allowed in school?

❑ Yes, students have the right to choose what they eat and drink.

❑ No, school vending machines should be filled with healthy drinks and snacks.

What type of question is it? _____ Forced Choice _____ Why? I am only given the two choices written by the author. I'm forced to choose between the two.

Question #2. How should my school handle the long lunch lines? Rank from 1 to 4 ("1" = best and "4" = worst).

_____ Stagger the lunch times.

_____ Allow students to earn "Front of the Line" privileges.

_____ Create more server windows.

_____ Sell food in carts, as well as in cafeteria.

What type of question is it? _____ Why? _____

_____

Question #3. Which statement best describes how you feel about global warming?

A. I don't think it will happen.

B. People and governments should act now to try to prevent or prepare for it.

C. The world may change, but living creatures will adapt.

D. There's nothing we can do about it.

What type of question is it? _____ Why? _____

_____

Question #4. What are the ways you need to prepare your home for a new pet?

What type of question is it? _____ Why? _____

_____

- -

Teacher Note: Fold this section under to cover it before making copies.

Answers: **2.** Rank Order; **3.** Forced Choice; **4.** Open Ended

Give an Oral Presentation

Great speakers don't just wing it and hope for the best. They know where they are going to start, where they are going to end, and how long it will take to get there.

Directions: It is time to present your topic to the class. In minutes, you will need to be able to explain why your topic would make for a valuable school subject that should be taught. Use the next few pages to assist you in completing this task.

❖ On this page, you will find a helpful "Presentation Reminders" card that you can use on the day of your speech to help keep you focused and on track.

❖ On the next page, you will find many tips to help you time your presentation.

❖ On the third page, you will find a template for your presentation.

Begin by writing an outline of your presentation. Base this outline on the lesson plan you have already created. Once you've written your outline, then the real rehearsals begin. Use the reminder card below to help you practice your speech. You can also bring it up to the front of the class with you and put it where you can see it as you speak.

Presentation Reminders

Volume

Can your audience (your *whole* audience) hear you? Remember to **speak loudly** enough so that the person at the back of the room can hear you.

Emphasis

Are your words flat and monotone, or is there emotion in your voice? How many "um"s, "er"s, or moments of silence are there in your presentation? Are you mumbling? Remember to **speak clearly** and show emotion.

Stance

Are you leaning, fidgeting, or rocking? Remember to **stand up straight**.

Eye Contact

Are you connecting with your audience with your eyes? Or are your eyes trapped to your cue cards and notes? Remember to **look at people** in different parts of the room.

Content

Did you do your research and are you communicating that research? Remember to **stay on topic**.

Timing

Are you speeding? Remember to **speak as if you're telling a story**.

Give an Oral Presentation *(cont.)*

The issue of timing is an important one when you are speaking in front of an audience. It takes rehearsing your oral presentation over and over—in front of a mirror, for your family, or maybe for your friends.

If you were to write an entire speech out on an 8½" x 11" piece of paper, the general rule of thumb is as follows: ***1 minute of speech = about ¾ of a page of handwriting***

So if you were doing a 3-minute presentation, you would be writing about a 4-page monologue. (If 3 = ¾ times x, then x = 4.) The challenge is to become so familiar with your speech that you don't need to memorize a written essay. Instead, write an outline, and then practice until your presentation times out right every time you practice.

Directions: Below is an activity that will aid you in timing out your presentation perfectly. Follow the steps provided.

Step 1

Create an outline of your content. Base this outline on your lesson plan.

Step 2

Use a timer.

Step 3

Stand up and use this worksheet as a guide while you time your presentation one section at a time.

Step 4

Slow down! Don't be nervous, and be sure to stay in control of your speed rather than the speed being in control of you. It might feel weird, but do it in slow motion once all the way through. Then try it again at a normal pace. This will help you avoid going too fast.

Step 5

With each attempt, write down your time next to the section to indicate your speed and pacing. Get it consistent, and you're ready to go.

Step 6

Repeat. Do it over and over until you don't need the timer to tell you how long you are spending on each section.

Give an Oral Presentation *(cont.)*

Directions: Below is one possible oral presentation broken down into sections. Divide your presentation into sections, and time each section using the template below.

Hook

    1st time through: _____   2nd time through: _____

Did you slow down with each rehearsal? Circle your response.   **YES**   **NO**

Background Information

    1st time through: _____   2nd time through: _____

Did you slow down with each rehearsal? Circle your response.   **YES**   **NO**

Main Content

    1st time through: _____   2nd time through: _____

Did you slow down with each rehearsal? Circle your response.   **YES**   **NO**

Questions & Answers (practice with someone asking you questions and you responding)

    1st time through: _____   2nd time through: _____

Did you slow down with each rehearsal? Circle your response.   **YES**   **NO**

Administer Quiz (Giving instructions)

    1st time through: _____   2nd time through: _____

Did you slow down with each rehearsal? Circle your response.   **YES**   **NO**

At the end of each full presentation, add your totals together.

    1st time through: _____   2nd time through: _____

Reflection

❖ Which was your best time? _____

❖ Why do you think it went better than the other times?_____

Write a Persuasive Letter

One of the most important elements to include in a "Teach the Teacher" unit is a persuasive business letter to a school administrator. Remember, the point of all of your research, writing, and lesson planning has been to develop an imaginary elective for the next school year. Now you just have to put all those skills together.

Directions: On a separate piece of paper, write a business letter to convince an administrator that your topic would make for a worthwhile class. Remember your writing skills, remember your audience, and remember to be persuasive.

Follow this format:

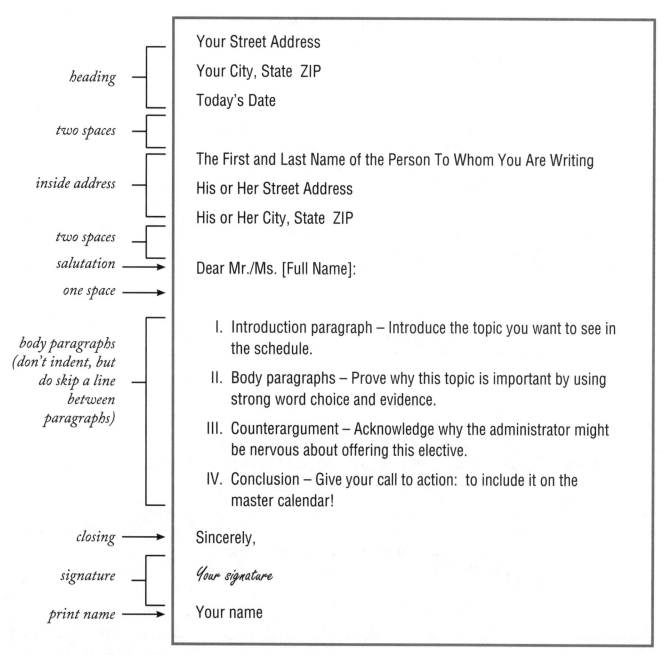

heading —
Your Street Address

Your City, State ZIP

Today's Date

two spaces —

inside address —
The First and Last Name of the Person To Whom You Are Writing

His or Her Street Address

His or Her City, State ZIP

two spaces —

salutation → Dear Mr./Ms. [Full Name]:

one space →

body paragraphs (don't indent, but do skip a line between paragraphs) —

  I. Introduction paragraph – Introduce the topic you want to see in the schedule.

  II. Body paragraphs – Prove why this topic is important by using strong word choice and evidence.

  III. Counterargument – Acknowledge why the administrator might be nervous about offering this elective.

  IV. Conclusion – Give your call to action: to include it on the master calendar!

closing → Sincerely,

signature — *Your signature*

print name → Your name

Unit Checklist

Below is a possible checklist for the "Teach the Teacher" unit. It should help to organize your time and work as you move through the process of creating a full project. Look ahead on your checklist and never lose sight of deadlines!

Genre	Description	Due	Turned In
1. Persuasive Writing	Write a persuasive business letter to your teacher pitching your topic.		
2. Lesson Plan	This is a step-by-step description of what you will teach, what you will need, and the activities that you will be doing with the class.		
3. Quiz	A 10-question assessment using various questioning strategies that the class will take and you will grade. (The score will not be counted against the students. You will score their quizzes as an assignment grade that goes towards your final score.)		
4. Bibliography	Include a works-cited page using correct bibliographical format.		
5. Oral Presentation	This will be scored using the oral-presentation rubric.		
6. Visual or Kinesthetic Element of Presentation	This can be an activity you are asking the students to do or a visual element used during your lesson plan (poster, PowerPoint, props, etc.).		
7. Container	How are you going to present your project? What will it look like?		

Unit 2: Persuasive-Writing Project

Teacher Instructions

The aim of this unit is to encourage students to connect school life to real life. With the Persuasive-Writing Project, students choose a topic to study and the format in which they want to present their results. These topics can be based on current issues that have an impact on the world around the students. After all, even elementary-school students can strive to make an impact on the world around them.

This unit includes the following components:

❖ **"Consider Cause and Effect"** (page 74) — Get students thinking about causes and their effects. This will help them examine the impacts their topics can have on the world.

❖ **"Choosing a Topic"** (page 75) — Have students begin to narrow down their choices for a topic that interests them. (Note: You may want to distribute three or more copies of the worksheet on page 75 so students can fill them out for multiple topics.)

❖ **"Write a Thesis Statement** (pages 76–77) — Show how a thesis statement functions in a persuasive essay and have students create thesis statements about their topics.

❖ **"The Newspaper Article"** (pages 78–79) — Review the parts of a newspaper article and have students think about those elements in relation to their topics.

❖ **"Show, Don't Tell"** (pages 80–81) — Discuss the functions of graphs and examine two prevalent types (the bar graph and the pie chart).

❖ **"Conduct an Interview"** (pages 82–84) — Teach the importance of getting information from people who are knowledgeable about a topic. These pages provide valuable tips and practice preparing for and conducting a great interview.

❖ **"Unit Checklist** (page 85) — This valuable resource keeps students focused, on task, and in front of deadlines.

Begin by getting your students comfortable with sifting through the news. Pick four students each week to bring in an article, blog post, etc., on topics that are important to them, their community, their country, etc. Collect the articles and keep them organized in a student-created resource library. The students can then begin choosing topics by searching through what's already in the classroom.

As students begin the unit and start to narrow down their choices for topics, have them consider the following questions:
❖ Is there a topic out there that is newsworthy?
❖ Are there at least two sides to the issue?
❖ Can I offer a solution or ask my reader/audience to do something to help the issue?

Have students consider all sources — books, websites, videos, podcasts, interviews, etc. — when researching their topics. Also, remind them to maintain a bibliography of their sources.

Consider Cause and Effect

It's important to understand that when an action takes place, there are always consequences. In other words, when something happens, there are results that occur because of that happening. This is called "cause and effect." Here is an example:

Action (Cause)

A student studies hard.

Consequence (Effect)

The student does well on his or her test.

Directions: The chart below gives some causes and some effects. Fill in blank boxes with appropriate responses. There are not necessarily any right or wrong answers. Just think about what makes sense.

Cause	Effect
A boy sneezes and doesn't cover his mouth.	
	The creatures in the oceans begin to die.
More people begin sharing rides to work every day.	
	Everywhere we walk, we get gum on our shoes.
With every "A" earned, a student gets $1 from the school's program.	

Take a look at the topics below. Decide if you are interested in discovering more about their causes and/or effects. Circle the ones that interest you most.

- traffic
- rainforests
- arts in schools
- dissecting animals

- money for attendance or grades
- commercials aimed at children
- dress codes in schools

- gum chewing
- cell phones in schools
- texting
- earning allowance

Choosing a Topic

Directions: It's time to choose a topic that is important and interesting to you. Fill out the following worksheet for a subject that you might want to focus on. Choose a topic that you think you will enjoy learning about.

Topic: _____

List three facts you already know about this topic:

   1. _____

   2. _____

   3. _____

Now, list one PRO (positive thing) about the topic and one CON (negative thing) about it.

Pro: _____

Con: _____

Next, answer the following questions about the topic:

   1. Why is this issue important? Why should your audience learn about it?_____

   _____

   _____

   2. Why are you interested in this topic? How do you think you relate to it?_____

   _____

   _____

Finally, think about the effects of this topic. Who does it impact? Is it important to the entire world or just your school or town? Write your answer on the lines below.

_____

_____

_____

Write a Thesis Statement

For this project, you will be writing an essay that attempts to persuade your readers to see your side of the topic you have chosen. And in this essay, the most important sentence may very well be the thesis statement.

That's because the thesis statement states your opinion and then it gives your most important reason for believing the way you do.

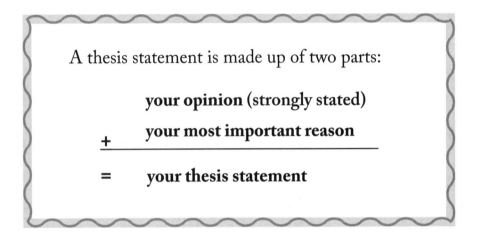

A thesis statement is made up of two parts:

your opinion (strongly stated)

+ **your most important reason**
_____

= **your thesis statement**

So, if you were to write a paper on why you should be able to drink water in class, the thesis statement might read as follows:

I strongly believe we should be able to keep a water bottle at our desks in class because drinking water keeps us hydrated during the day.

Now, looking at the sentence above, the reader knows what the author's opinion is and why the author thinks that way.

Directions: Write a new thesis statement about water bottles in the classroom. This time, write the statement from the point of view of someone who is against allowing students to have water bottles at their desks. That might not be your personal opinion, but it is important to be able to present an argument, even if you don't agree with it.

_____

_____

_____

Write a Thesis Statement *(cont.)*

Directions: Look at the thesis statements below. For each one, do the following:

- ❖ Underline the phrase that states the author's opinion.
- ❖ Draw a box around the phrase that gives the author's reason for feeling the way he or she does.

Thesis Statement #1

We should definitely not pay students for grades because it does not teach students to be motivated from the inside.

Thesis Statement #2

There should be a stop sign at the corner of 1st and Main because people race dangerously around the block.

Thesis Statement #3

We should start an energy-saving program at our school because it will save money on the school's electrical bills.

Directions: Now think about a possible thesis statement for the topic you've chosen. Fill in as much information as you can before writing your thesis statement below.

Your topic: _____

Your opinion: _____

Your most important reason: _____

_____

Your thesis statement: _____

_____

_____

The Newspaper Article

A newspaper or online article is a great way to give the facts about your topic, without any bias or opinion. It can also be a little project all by itself: these articles combine writing, photographs, graphs, interviews, etc. But before you can put all of those elements into a final product, you need know how to write the actual article first.

A newspaper article has a specific structure. It typically has five parts:

1. **Headline** — This is the title of your article. It quickly grabs the reader's attention and tells him or her what the article is about.

2. **Byline** — This names the author of the article.

3. **Lead Section** — These intro paragraphs tell the reader the most important parts of the story. The first paragraph contains a *hook* to grab the reader's attention. This section continues with the "Five Ws and One H" (Who, What, When, Where, Why, and How) about the subject.

4. **Expansion** — These are the next few paragraphs that build on the first paragraphs. This is where the reader can learn about what people have said about the topic. Perhaps there are details like quotes or data to back up the topic of the article.

5. **Related Information** — This includes additional information that might prove interesting to the reader but that isn't important to understanding the initial purpose of the article.

① **Slinger Is Pitch Perfect**

② By Marcy Jones
    Staff Writer

③ Oak View Junior High pitcher Scott Slinger threw 7 perfect innings against Wilson Junior High on Thursday. The 11-year-old hurler allowed no hits and no walks, and he struck out 20 Warriors. Slinger's perfect game was the first in Kent County since John Willis accomplished the feat in 1984.

④ "Scotty was really sharp today," beamed Acorns coach Tom Peters. "I kidded him about missing that 21st strikeout, though." The Wilson Warriors were able to muster just one batted ball, a pop fly out in the 4th inning. When asked about his performance, Slinger just smiled and said, "I guess I had a good game."

⑤ Next Thursday, the Acorns will take on their rivals, Jefferson Junior High, in an important game. Both teams are 8–3.

The Newspaper Article *(cont.)*

Directions: Go online and find a news article on an appropriate webpage. A good place to look would be *http://www.cnn.com/studentnews/*. Click on an article that you may be interested in. Cut and paste it into a word-processing document. Then do the following:

1. Use the features in your word-processing program to highlight certain elements of the article according to the color code below:

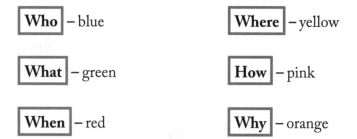

Who – blue	**Where** – yellow
What – green	**How** – pink
When – red	**Why** – orange

2. Then, underline the hook.

3. Next, read through the article again and **boldface** any quotes or other evidence that serves as details for the topic.

Directions: Once you have researched the topic you have chosen for your project, write an outline for a newspaper article on your topic. Include the headline and also the information you will put in the lead section and in the expansion section.

Rules to Remember

When thinking about your news article, remember these three rules of thumb for journalism:

1. **No bias.**

   Only stick to the facts; don't include your opinion for one side or the other. As a writer, pretend that you are the news anchor, just reporting the facts.

2. **Pick a position and stick to it.**

   Decide the article's point of view and don't drift from it.

3. **Keep it simple and unemotional.**

   Many writing elements — like metaphors, similes, emotion, visualization, concrete description, or personal experience — are not suited to a news article.

Show, Don't Tell

You've probably heard the saying, "A picture is worth a thousand words." Well, sometimes it is true that an image can do more to convince a reader than only words would do. Sometimes telling isn't enough. Showing your reader what you are saying is the best way to make it clear. Graphs provide a great way to do just that.

You can begin by creating a question to ask of classmates, neighbors, family members, etc. Once you collect the results, a graph can show your findings in a picture that is easily understood in a glance.

Now what kind of graph should you use? Well, there are many different formats for graphing, but two of the most common are the bar graph and the pie chart.

Bar Graphs

A *bar graph* uses rectangular bars to show the values of the things they represent. Bar graphs are great for showing the difference between values.

Directions: Look at the data given for a project called "The Sticking Point with Gum in School." Use the results to fill in the bars on the graph below. The first bar has been done for you.

Students Polled: 33

Question: "What do you do with gum when you're done chewing?"

Results (in number of students):

"I don't chew gum." = **6**   "I swallow it." = **9**

"I throw it in the trash." = **15**   "I spit it on the ground." = **3**

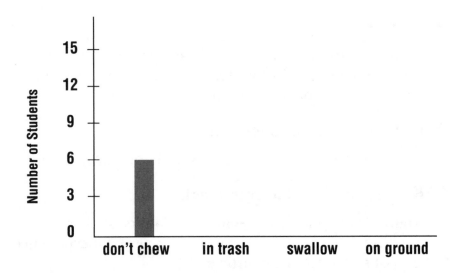

Show, Don't Tell *(cont.)*

A *pie chart* is in the shape of a circle that is divided into sections. Pie charts are great for showing big differences when your data has a wide range.

Directions: Look at the data given for a project called "The Trouble with TV." Use the results to label the sections of the pie chart below.

Students Polled: 80

Question: "How much television do you watch each week?"

Results (in number of students):

10 hours or more = **60**   1–4 hours = **6**

5–9 hours = **12**   I don't watch TV. = **2**

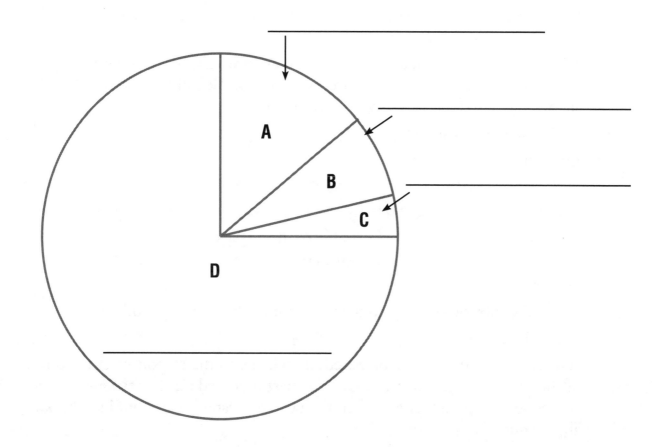

Directions: Create your own poll and convert your results into a bar graph or pie chart. Try using a spreadsheet program (for example, Excel) to create a quick 3-D graph. Add the results into a newspaper article or some other part of your final project.

Conduct an Interview

For a research project, you can interview anyone who can give you some information that you wouldn't be able to find out in a book or online. You want the subject to respond in a unique way you wouldn't find anywhere else.

To get a great interview takes planning. There are two stages to conducting an interview. Here are tips to help you get the most out of both of those stages:

Interviewing Tips
The Preparation

☞ Research your topic thoroughly.

☞ Research your interview subject and how he or she relates to your topic.

☞ Come prepared with a pen and paper, or better yet, a way to record the subject's voice.

☞ Come to the interview with a list of at least 10 questions. Make sure they are not "yes" or "no" questions.

☞ When you initially contact the person for an interview, don't assume that he or she has the time or the desire to meet you. Be polite and ask if he or she would be so kind as to give you some time.

☞ Arrive dressed for success.

☞ Be on time.

Interviewing Tips
The Actual Interview

☞ Use eye contact.

☞ Shake the interviewee's hand in greeting and when saying goodbye.

☞ Say, "Thank you."

☞ Ask a question that you've prepared, then listen to the response. A good rule of thumb would be to ask a follow-up question based on the response. This proves you are paying attention to the person's response and not just thinking about your next question.

☞ When the interview is over, go somewhere where you can write/type everything that you remember, even if you've recorded the interview. Note the person's clothes, the room, and the walls — everything that can serve to set a scene for those who read your interview.

Conduct an Interview *(cont.)*

In this activity, you are going to practice asking follow-up questions based on an answer. Let's pretend that you're interviewing the principal of your school. Here is a question you may ask at some point during the interview:

> "What do you think about the idea of paying students to come to school?"

The principal answers:

> "Well, I guess good grades are a form of payment, right? The way I see it, if a student doesn't come to school, then he or she won't have an opportunity to earn that good grade. Paying students for doing the minimum — just showing up — doesn't help them. When I was a student, my parents would pay me a quarter for every "A" I got, but my school wasn't involved in that reward. I would worry if schools had to be involved in that kind of praise."

Directions: Based on the principal's response, develop three questions you could ask to prove that you were listening to the response.

1. _____

   _____

   _____

2. _____

   _____

   _____

Conduct an Interview *(cont.)*

After you have conducted an interview, you should follow up your interview within a day with a more formal "thank you" to the person for granting you the interview.

Directions: Imagine that you have interviewed a professor at a local college on his/her knowledge of the history of your city. Below are fields for an e-mail that you are sending to thank the professor for granting you the interview and giving you some of his/her time and insights into the subject.

Be sure to include: a greeting, a reminder of the interview, and a mention of one of the professor's points that was particularly helpful. End the e-mail by thanking the professor again and signing off with your full name.

To: _____

From: _____

Subject: _____

Unit Checklist

Below is a possible checklist for the "Persuasive Writing" unit. It should help to organize your time and work as you move through the process of creating a full project. Look ahead on your checklist and never lose sight of deadlines!

Genre	Description	Due	Turned In
1. Persuasive Writing	Write a business letter to your teacher in order to pitch the project.		
2. Research	Complete Cornell notes. Include at least two separate sources.		
3. Narrative	Write a short story based on your topic.		
4. Bibliography	Include a works-cited page. Use the correct format.		
5. News Article	Write an article about your topic. Include a visual element (photo, graph, etc.).		
6. Poem	Write a poem in any format. Use figurative language and poetic devices.		
7. Your Choice	Choose an additional genre to depict your topic.		

Unit 3: Create-a-State Project

Teacher Instructions

Most state projects ask students to study their state and regurgitate what they've learned. But the highest form of comprehension is not in being able to remember (after all, we live in the age of the search engines, right?), but in being able to create something from the information we understand. Researching a state is one thing, but imagining a new state is another, far-more creative endeavor. In 4th grade, students become experts of the state they live in. This unit will take this idea one step further and ask them to create the 51st state in America.

This is going to take a little time, some knowledge about their own state and the characteristics about states in general, and a lot of imagination.

This unit includes the following components:

❖ **"The State You Call Home"** (page 87) — Begin this unit by having students research the state in which they live. This will focus students as they begin thinking about the states they will create and the questions they will need to answer about those states.

❖ **"All About Maps"** (pages 88–89) — Use these pages to show students the elements involved in mapping. This activity will lead up to the creation of a 51st state by each student.

❖ **"Put Your State on the Map"** (pages 90–91) — Have students show how their newly created states fit into the existing map of the U.S. Then have them create a more detailed look at their state's topographical features.

❖ **"Introducing the 51st State"** (pages 92–93) — This is where students really get to fill in the details of their states. Two pages of questions about their new states give students an opportunity for creative thinking.

❖ **"History at a Glance"** (page 94) — Students use the timeline format to show the history of their state, from its early beginnings to its present condition.

❖ **"A Great Place to Visit!"** (page 95) — Through the creation of travel brochures, each student will have the opportunity to convince readers why his or her state is the place to visit. A travel brochure serves a great project-based writing activity because it combines genres by incorporating visuals, narratives, and facts all in one handy folded document.

❖ **"Unit Checklist"** (page 96) — This valuable resource helps students stay focused, on task, and in front of deadlines.

The State You Call Home

In this project, you are going to get the chance to create a brand new state. First, though, it makes sense to learn a little bit about what makes a state what it is. And what better place to start than with the state in which you live?

Directions: Answer the questions below about the state in which you live. As you do this, think about the state you will be creating. How will it be similar to your home state? How will it be different?

My Home State

General Information

1. What is the name of your home state? _____

2. What does your state's flag look like? Draw it in the box.

3. Who is your state's governor? _____

4. About how many people live in your state? _____

5. In what year did your state become part of the U.S.? _____

Geography

1. Where in the U.S. is your state located (for example, Midwest, East Coast)?

   _____

2. Which, if any, other states border your state? _____

3. Which, if any, foreign countries border your state? _____

4. What are some notable topographical features of your state (for example, mountain ranges, deserts, canyons, rivers)? _____

   _____

Visitor Information

1. What are some popular tourist destinations in your state? _____

   _____

2. Name any foods for which your state is known. _____

3. Name any popular sports teams that call your state home. _____

   _____

All About Maps

Maps are all around us. You can find a map of a country, a state, a town — even your school. A map is a great way to give a reader a visual glimpse of an area.

Think about your classroom. From your perspective sitting at a desk, it may be hard to get a full picture of the entire classroom. But a map, drawn from the perspective of a bird looking down, can do just that. Such a map might look something like this:

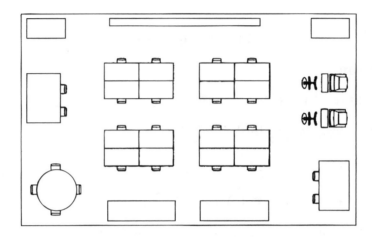

Directions: In the space below, map your classroom. Draw it from a bird's-eye view, just as in the example above.

Now that you have mapped something relatively small, it's time to take that same idea and use it to map something much larger. Continue on to the activity on page 89.

All About Maps *(cont.)*

When you are mapping large areas, it becomes necessary to use symbols. After all, if you're mapping something the size of a classroom, you can draw most of the main elements in that classroom. You can draw computers and desks and bookshelves. If you're drawing something the size of a city or state or country, there is no way you can include realistic drawings of the parts in it. When you are mapping a state, even something as large as a major city must be reduced down to the size of a dot.

That's where certain map tools can help you:

❖ **Key** — A key explains how to read your map. Inside the key are symbols, along with a brief description of what those symbols mean.

❖ **Symbols** — These appear in both the key and on the map itself. They are the best way to visually represent something that is big and important in the real world but cannot take up much space on the map.

❖ **Compass** — A compass helps the reader understand how to read the map. It shows which direction is north, south, east, or west.

Directions: Look at the map below. On each blank line, write the name of the element shown. Use the descriptions above to help you.

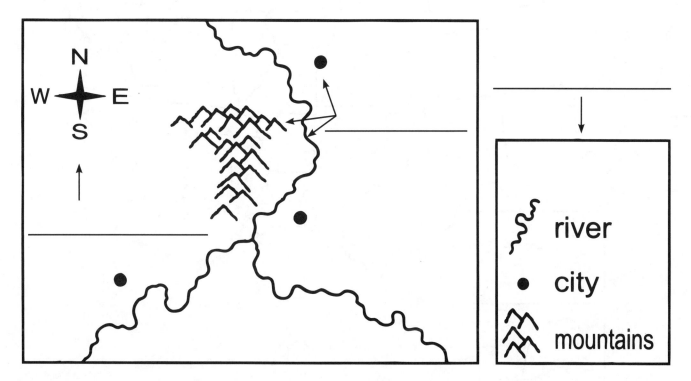

Now that have learned about the state in which you live and about how to read maps, it's time to create your own state and put it on a map.

Put Your State on the Map

Directions: Here is a map of the United States. Imagine there is a 51st state. You can put it anywhere, and you can make it any shape you want. On the map below, sketch in an outline of your state. Will it be connected to the U.S. mainland or embedded within another state? Or will it be detached from the mainland, like Alaska and Hawaii?

Now is also the time to unveil the name of your state. Write it here:

_____

Put Your State on the Map *(cont.)*

On the previous page, you showed us where your state fits on a map of the United States. Now is the time to show your state in lot more detail.

Directions: Map your state in the space below. Be sure to include the following elements:

❖ a key

❖ symbols (for cities, rivers, lakes, mountains, tourist attractions, etc.)

❖ a compass

Name of State _____

Introducing the 51st State

Now that we know where your state is located, it's time to give us an idea of what life is like in the 51st state.

Directions: Fill in the form below and on page 93. Use these forms as a way to record all of the facts and bits of information about your imaginary state.

The 51st State of the United States of America

1. What is the name of your state? _____

2. Where did your state's name come from, and/or what does it mean?

   _____

   _____

3. How many people live in your state? _____

4. What is the name of your state's capital city? _____

5. What are the names of its three largest cities? _____

   _____

6. What is the name of your state's governor? _____

7. What does your state flag look like? Please sketch it here:

Please continue filling out the form on page 93.

Introducing the 51st State *(cont.)*

8. What is your state's motto? _____

9. Write the first four lines of your state song below.

_____

_____

_____

_____

10. What are the natural resources that can be found in your state? _____

_____

11. In what year was your state first colonized/explored? _____

12. What is the food your state is known for? _____

_____

13. What popular tourist attractions is your state known for? _____

_____

14. Do any popular sports teams call your state home? If so, give their names.

_____

15. Finally, give two facts about your state that make it unique to this country.

_____

_____

_____

History at a Glance

A timeline is a visual representation of a period in history. It can include numbers, words, and drawings. It gives a quick glance at what happened and when.

Directions: Imagine how your 51st state was founded. Who discovered it? Who first crossed into its borders? Were there people living there first, or did explorers discover its resources? Why did those who came there travel all that way? Think about these questions and more as you fill in the rough draft of your state's timeline below.

Hints: In each small box above the timeline, write the year or date something happened. In each large box below the timeline, write a description or draw a picture of the event that occurred on that date.

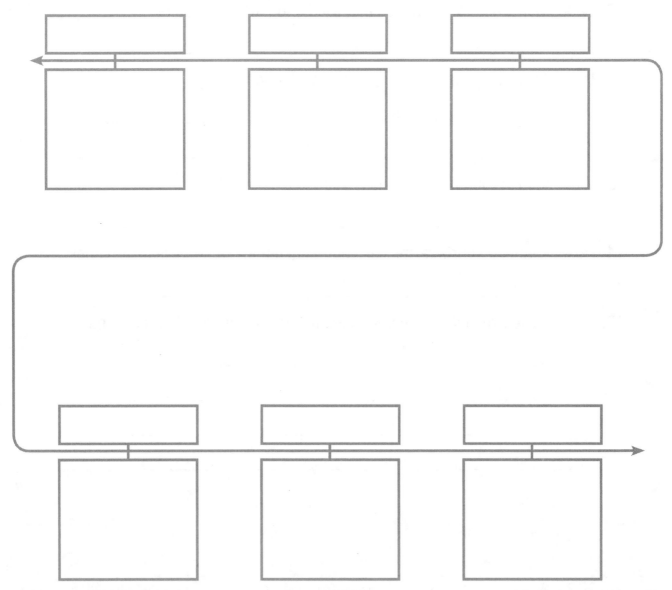

A Great Place to Visit!

When tourists go on vacation to an unfamiliar place, they often look at travel brochures in order to find out more information about that place. Brochures are like handy reference guides that tell them about places to go, locations to visit, facts about the area, and restaurants to try. Best of all, the wealth of information found on a travel brochure can be folded up and fit conveniently into a pocket for easy reference.

Directions: It's time to create a travel brochure for your state. It all starts simply with a piece of 8½" x 11" paper folded to look like the image to the right:

Here are some guidelines to follow as you create your travel brochure:

On the front . . .

❖ Write the name of the state and its capital city.

❖ Include a drawing, photo, or other visual that represents the state.

On the inside . . .

❖ Include information that will grab your reader's attention and really convince him or her to visit your state:

• unique places to see

• facts about the state

• facts about the largest cities

• reasons why the state is a
  great place to visit

• quotes from visitors and citizens

• restaurants to try

• pastimes to enjoy

• sports teams to watch

As you fill in the details of your brochure, remember to use persuasive word choices. After all, you are trying to build excitement and interest in your new state. You are trying to show why it is a great destination spot for travelers.

Unit Checklist

Below is a possible checklist for the "Create a State" unit. It should help to organize your time and work as you move through the process of creating a full project. Look ahead on your checklist and never lose sight of deadlines!

Genre	Description	Due	Turned In
1. Research	Complete Cornell notes. Include two separate sources.		
2. Map	Complete a map of your imaginary state. Include a key, symbols, and a compass.		
3. Fact Page	Submit a completed form that gives all of the general information about your mythical state.		
4. Narrative	Set a story in your new state, and give a first-hand account of the state's early history.		
5. Timeline	Fill in a timeline that gives a glimpse of the important events that have shaped the history of your state.		
6. Brochure	Create a tourist brochure designed to persuade tourists to visit your state.		
7. Your Choice	Choose an additional genre to depict your topic.		